Devil's Advocates

DEVIL'S ADVOCATES is a series of books devoted to exploring the classics of horror cinema. Contributors to the series come from the fields of teaching, academia, journalism and fiction, but all have one thing in common: a passion for the horror film and a desire to share it with the widest possible audience.

'The admirable Devil's Advocates series is not only essential – and fun – reading for the serious horror fan but should be set texts on any genre course.'
Dr Ian Hunter, Reader in Film Studies, De Montfort University, Leicester

'Auteur Publishing's new Devil's Advocates critiques on individual titles... offer bracingly fresh perspectives from passionate writers. The series will perfectly complement the BFI archive volumes.' **Christopher Fowler, *Independent on Sunday***

'Devil's Advocates has proven itself more than capable of producing impassioned, intelligent analyses of genre cinema... quickly becoming the go-to guys for intelligent, easily digestible film criticism.' ***Horror Talk.com***

'Auteur Publishing continue the good work of giving serious critical attention to significant horror films.' ***Black Static***

 DevilsAdvocatesbooks

 DevilsAdBooks

T0323737

DEVIL'S ADVOCATES

THE WITCH

BRANDON GRAFIUS

ACKNOWLEDGEMENTS

I've been deeply grateful for the chance to spend the last couple of years immersed in this challenging film. Thanks to John Atkinson for accepting my proposal for this *Devil's Advocates* volume, and allowing me to spend some time trying to unpack some of its secrets. I also offer thanks to the anonymous reader, whose detailed comments and suggestions have led to a much improved volume.

First published in 2020 by
Auteur, an imprint of
Liverpool University Press,
4 Cambridge Street,
Liverpool
L69 7ZU

Series design: Nikki Hamlett at Cassels Design
Set by Cassels Design www.casselsdesign.co.uk
Printed and bound by CPI Group (UK) Ltd, Croydon CR0 4YY

British Library Cataloguing-in-Publication Data
A catalogue record for this book is available from the British Library

ISBN paperback: 978-1-80034-805-9
ISBN hardback: 978-1-80034-835-6
ISBN pdf: 978-1-80034-604-8
ISBN epub: 978-1-80034-771-7

CONTENTS

INTRODUCTION

When it made its premiere at the 2015 Sundance Film Festival, *The Witch* left its audience stunned by its slow building, tension-filled storyline, its evocative use of American history and folklore, and its enigmatic ending. *The Witch* was one of the surprise hits of the year's festival, and it left with a prestigious distribution contract in place. The hype train ran downhill a bit too fast for the film's wide release, leaving audiences split as to whether they had seen something amazing or just underwhelming. But after the dust settled, and the film could be evaluated outside of the marketing buzz, *The Witch* quickly built a reputation as one of the decade's richest horror films.

This monograph will read *The Witch* through a variety of lenses. After a brief introduction, it will dig into the film's finely detailed historical background. Particular attention will be paid attention to the religious controversies that provide the impetus for the family's expulsion from their colony, and serve as the backdrop for their personal struggles with the malevolent forces which may lurk in the woods, or may reside closer to home. We'll look at the generic connections of the film, and see how it fits into the increasingly well-populated genre of folk horror. And we'll talk about the folkloric background of the film, including how it uses the Devil, witchcraft, and New England legends. This will lead us to an exploration of the film's setting and characters, arguing that much of the film's tension arises from the interwoven character arcs that we see emerging from the family members, and the conflict that ensues when they are faced with a hostile environment threatening them from without as well as a family structure that is crumbling around them. And we'll take a quick journey through some theory-laden approaches, testing whether the idea of a laughing medusa can help us read the film's audience-dividing conclusion. As Hélène Cixous (1976) has pointed out in her famous essay, one of the most frightening things the male mind can conceive of is a powerful, laughing female.

My personal experience with *The Witch* involved admiring the film on first watching, while at the same time finding it slower moving than I wished, with an ending that left me feeling unsatisfied. But I found myself returning to it over and over again in my mind in the coming weeks, until I felt the need to watch it again. The second time through, I was pulled into the dynamics of this struggling family, the menace of the woods, the deep connections with questions of faith, and the immersive period set design. The film's powerful, unrelenting feeling of slowly building dread calls to mind such isolation-fueled classics as *The Thing* (1982) and *The Shining* (1980). And the multiple layers of subtext left it simmering in my mind for weeks afterwards. There was enough going on in my head around this film that I pitched an article on it, reading it in combination with the similarly themed family-in-isolation film *It Comes at Night*. But after several months of wrestling with these films for this article, I still didn't feel like I was done with *The Witch*. This monograph is the product of that feeling – being continually drawn back to a film that wouldn't let me go, because I kept finding there was more in it to discover.

ROBERT EGGERS

Writer-director Robert Eggers was born in 1983, and grew up in New Hampshire. His first professional experience was as a production designer for experimental theatre in New York City. By the time he turned to film, he had quite a bit of theatrical design experience under his belt. He directed a pair of short films in the late '00's, *Hansel and Gretel* and *The Tell-Tale Heart*, both of which he was able to use to obtain financing for a full-length feature. After several screenplays that weren't able to find monetary backing, Eggers' screenplay of *The Witch* managed to attract the attention of production company Parts and Labor.

The Witch was Eggers' first feature as writer-director, though he had written and directed shorts, and served as the production designer for the 2013 feature *Spirit Cabinet* (dir. Jay Stern). His background in production design serves *The Witch* extremely well, as the period detail adds tremendously to the sense that we are actually living inside of a Puritan's nightmare. Along with crafting the family's dwellings by hand, Eggers wanted only period instruments for the soundtrack. His eye for detail even extended to his characters' corsets, which he insisted be made of period-accurate wool, rather than the bone corsets that are usually used in Hollywood films (Murphy, 2016). Eggers has referred to *The Witch* as '*The Revenant*, Jr.', in reference to the notoriously grueling shooting of Alejandro González Iñárritu's brutal epic of revenge in Colonial America (Ifeanyi, 2016). Eggers worked on the film for over four years, including significant time spent researching the times, customs, and religion of Puritan New England (Duca, 2016).

The homestead, in all its period-detailed glory (© A24)

Eggers' desire for period detail even extends to the film's title. The film is technically called *The Witch*, to imitate the substitution of two v's for w's that was common in 17th century printing.[1] However, this monograph will refer to the title as *The Witch* for simplicity's sake.

The film premiered at the 2015 Sundance Film Festival. While Sundance isn't known for being a horror-friendly festival, *The Witch* was awarded the Best Director (in the U.S. Dramatic category) prize, and was nominated for a Grand Jury Prize (also U.S. Dramatic). Eggers left the festival with plenty of buzz, and a distribution deal for the film with A24. *The Witch* premiered in US theatres on Feb. 19th, 2016, and on March 11th in the UK.

Eggers' second feature, *The Lighthouse* (co-written with his brother Max), premiered at the 2019 Cannes Festival as part of the Directors' Fortnight slate. Upcoming projects may or may not include a medieval epic called *The Knight* and a remake of *Nosferatu* (also with Anya Taylor-Joy), both of which have been associated with the production company Studio 8.

SYNOPSIS

As the movie opens, William (Ralph Ineson) is on trial in a New England courthouse. While his heresy is unstated, William believes himself to be in the right, and will not repent. He and his family are banished from the colony as a result. They depart, and find a patch of land to settle on.

The story resumes some time later, after the family has built a homestead. The family now consists of seven members: the patriarch William, mother Katherine (Kate Dickie), oldest daughter Thomasin (Anya Taylor-Joy), son Caleb (Harvey Scrimshaw), twins Jonas (Lucas Dawson) and Mercy (Ellie Grainger), and infant Samuel. Thomasin takes Samuel to the river to wash her father's clothes and engages in a game of peek-a-boo with him, but she opens her eyes to find him gone. Scouring the forest for him proves unsuccessful, and the family assumes he has been taken by a witch. The younger children, Jonas and Mercy, assume that Thomasin is in league with her; they also seem to have preternatural knowledge about Black Phillip, the family's goat.

The family strains under the weight of a poor harvest and isolation, blaming each other for faults both real and imagined. Thomasin and Caleb sneak off to check the traps for meat, but the family dog runs off after a rabbit. As Caleb gives chase, he stumbles upon a hut in the middle of the forest, and is beckoned within by a beautiful young woman. Thomasin returns to the homestead in the evening with Caleb still missing. The family argues about the proper course of action, but determines that William will go to the village in the morning to ask for help. But Caleb returns in the middle of the night, naked and stumbling through the rain. The family tries to nurse him back to health, but Caleb dies after yelling about the witch who came for him in the woods.

As the family hurls accusations of witchcraft at each other, William locks all of his surviving children into the barn for the night. When William checks on them in the morning, the barn door has been smashed open, and only Thomasin remains alive. Before he can process the events, he is gored by Black Phillip. Katherine arrives to find her husband dead; assuming Thomasin is to blame, she attacks her daughter. Thomasin kills her mother in self-defense. Left alone, she calls for Black Phillip, and is met by a devilish figure who asks her to sign his book. Thomasin agrees, and walks into the woods to join a witches' Sabbath.

OVERVIEW

The evidence points to there being little in the way of witchcraft being practiced in early modern Europe or Colonial America, unless one counts folk remedies (Cohn, 2000). For generations, scholars have agreed that the witch-hunts of Europe, Salem, and elsewhere were an unhealthy concoction of religious anxiety, fear of women, an attachment to ecclesiastical power, and all sorts of dangerous ideas mixed together into an unhealthy obsession. For example, Walter Stephens has argued that the European obsession with witches reveals an anxiety over the existence of God, brought about by the increasing prevalence of Enlightenment ideas (Stephens, 2003). As we'll see in our exploration of *The Witch*, religious anxiety is not far from the surface, and reveals itself in all sorts of horrifying ways. Benjamin Ray has argued that religion is at the heart of the Salem witch controversies, and that the anxieties over the role of the church in the colony's life is a cause that cannot be neglected in any study of the Salem witch trials (Ray 2010). While *The Witch* takes place several decades before the witch trials, these anxieties are deeply embedded in the film.

These religious and folkloric beliefs are foundational enough to *The Witch* that this monograph will spend a significant amount of time exploring them. After the introductory material, the monograph will continue with a brief history of Puritan religious beliefs, give a little history of the Massachusetts Bay Colony, and talk about some of the religious controversies that ran through the community, including the Salem witch trials of 1692. Before continuing on with the folkloric background, a chapter will explore *The Witch*'s literary and generic heritage, arguing that it fits most comfortably within the (still emerging) genre of folk horror, and that its particular brand of folk horror finds itself situated within the legends and stories of New England. From there, the next chapter will move to the folkloric elements of the movie, including offering some background on its conception of witches and the Devil. The chapter will also explore some of the animals who appear in the film, many of which have a long history of association with witches.

The book will then transition out of the film's background and into readings of the film itself. As much of the film is centered on the characters within the family and their complicated series of interrelations, the book will spend time discussing each character's arc, their challenges, and the frustrations that build within them. Through this exploration, the book will show how the overwhelming tension in the family builds throughout the film, before finally exploding with a crash of firewood. In the final chapter, we'll offer several additional readings of the film, including a focus on the audience-dividing ending. The conclusion will assess the film's influence, which already seems to be present only a few years after its release.

Overall, this monograph demonstrates that *The Witch* is a rich and deeply complex work of art, which rewards multiple viewings and even a little bit of research on the part of the viewer (though not necessarily the three years' worth that Eggers reportedly underwent!). A deep exploration of the film's context reveals a cast of multifaceted, three-dimensional characters, whose tragedy is their inability to live out their individual lives within the structures of their repressive religious and family environment. The movie's a wild ride, and one that only gets better once you've dived deeply into its background.

FOOTNOTES

1.   Proot 2014, 'Miracles lately vvrought,' gives a brief survey of the title page of 17th century folios printed in the Netherlands, and concludes that two 'v''s are used as a 'w' approximately 59% of the time.

THE PURITAN RELIGION OF NEW ENGLAND

BACKGROUND OF THE PURITAN MOVEMENT

Eggers takes the setting of *The Witch* very seriously. This is evident in the vast amount of research he reports having done for the film, and shows through in the film itself. An extremely important part of this setting is the Puritan religion of New England. The centrality of this religious background is evident in the opening of the film, and continues to serve as a driving force behind the family's anxieties and unraveling relationships. This section will provide a brief overview of the Puritan religion, particularly as it expressed itself in the 17th century Massachusetts Bay colony, with an eye towards the elements of Puritan religious beliefs which are most relevant to *The Witch*.

The Puritan movement grew out of the Protestant Reformation, the cataclysmic shock that split up the Catholic church in the 16th century and led to our modern denominations. Prior to the Reformation, the church was (relatively) unified in Western Europe under the authority of the Pope of Rome, although the Orthodox church of Eastern Europe had already split from the Catholic Church in the 11th century over issues of politics and doctrine. What would come to be known as the Reformation was launched when a pious German priest by the name of Martin Luther nailed his Ninety-Five Theses to the door of the church in Wittenberg in 1517.[1] While Luther wrote them in Latin, the language of scholarly discourse at the time, they were soon translated into German. (One of the key components of the Reformation would be the translation of biblical and ecclesiastical texts into the common language.) With the aid of the newly invented printing press, these theses circulated throughout Germany only a couple of months after Luther posting them, and spread into the rest of Western Europe.

At the heart of Luther's complaints was the issue of indulgences. The full title of Luther's thesis is actually *Ninety-Five Theses on the Power and Efficacy of Indulgences*, lest a reader might miss Luther's main point. Under this practice, the Catholic Church had determined that most sins could be forgiven after an act of penance; the most effective act of penance, coincidentally of course, was a donation to the Church. This system had become more and more widespread through the 15th and 16th centuries, leading to

The Wittenberg Church Door

outrageous abuses in which the pope would authorize individuals to sell indulgences in particular areas, on the condition that they gave a cut of the proceeds to the Church (González 2010: 26-28). Before snake oil or lightning rods, there was the travelling indulgence salesman. Really, some priests would travel door-to-door selling indulgences.

Luther's argument against this system was two-fold; his first argument was practical, his second theological. First, he considered the aspect of corruption unacceptable, and should be halted immediately. But secondly, Luther objected to the idea that forgiveness could be achieved through human actions of any sort, whether monetary gifts or a simple act of contrition. For Luther, forgiveness was never deserved, but was given as a gift of God's grace. (If you're familiar with the film, this might sound suspiciously similar to many of the prayers and teachings that William delivers to his family.) Luther didn't intend to break off from the Catholic church; he conceived of himself as merely correcting the errors of the Church, so that it could return to its true mission. But he soon found himself as the unwitting spokesperson for a new movement, as the simple theological ideas that he expounded ended up splitting the church in half, exposing the rifts that had been slowly building over the centuries. After decades of wars, public disputes, and ecclesiastical councils, the Church that had once been universal, at least in Western Europe, was fragmented into numerous movements and counter-movements.[2]

The Puritan movement emerged from this chaotic religious landscape, against the backdrop of the Reformation's effects in England. The Church of England was born out of a series of complicated disputes between Rome and England, largely concerning matters of both taxation and the status of the royal heirs. In short, King Henry VIII had been married multiple times, but the Catholic Church did not recognize divorce as legitimate, so they viewed his true heir as being the daughter of his first marriage – the young woman who would grow up to be known as Mary Tudor, and would eventually become the Queen of England in spite of her father's efforts. But Henry VIII wished to enter into another marriage that might result in a male heir to the throne, and Rome refused to issue him an annulment for the first marriage. Eventually, Parliament, in support of the King's wishes, declared the King to be the 'supreme head of the church of England', causing an irrevocable split between the Church of England and the Catholic Church.

Since the split between the Church of England and the Catholic church was primarily one of politics rather than theology, the Church of England still looked quite a bit like the Catholic Church. While elements of the Protestant Reformation seeped in from Germany, France, and the rest of the continent, for many in England the split between the Church of England and the Catholic Church did not go nearly far enough. There were theological disputes over the meaning and purpose of communion, the perpetuation of the church hierarchy, and the use of the Church of England's newly adopted *Book of Common Prayer*. But perhaps most importantly, these radical Protestant groups felt that the Church had strayed from true biblical teachings, allowing itself to become indulgent and morally lax. The Puritans wished both to continue the Reformation project begun by Luther, and also place a greater emphasis on the moral behavior of the believing individual.

A preacher in Oxfordshire, John Dod, preached a series of sermons on the Ten Commandments in the early part of the 17th century. His sermons focused not only on the grace that God offered to the elect, but on the changes in the individual this saving grace brought about. As historian Michael P. Winship describes Dod's message:

> ...after you had been justified and continued the strict self-examination that was a daily part of puritan spiritual practice, you would start to notice God creating changes in you, changes in your outward behavior, of course, but even more important changes in your feelings and states of mind: new love for God, a new spirit of prayer, newly heartfelt repentance when you caught yourself breaking one of God's commandments. (Winship 2018: 55)

These were all signs that an individual had been saved, and was destined for eternal glory rather than damnation. This would become a key theological idea of the Puritan movement. An individual's salvation or damnation was determined by God. ('Pre-destined', as Calvin would say.) There's nothing anyone can do to influence that decision. But an individual might have a hint as to whether they've been placed among the elect based on the feelings and states of mind that Dod describes. And of course, outward blessings, such as a healthy family life and success in business, can also be signs that an individual has been selected for salvation. So while we can't know the mind of God, we can continually check in with our own feelings for some hints. And we can keep a close eye on our neighbors, as well. This inability to know the will of God, coupled with a desperate worry over it, likely kept many a Puritan tossing and turning at night.

The Puritan movement started growing throughout the 16th century, but gathered more and more momentum during the early years of the 17th. While many of the Puritans would remain in England and agitate for governmental reform, leading to a Civil War and Oliver Cromwell's rise to power, others left for the newly colonized lands across the ocean to establish communities of their own. This flight from England to the colonies has been labelled 'The Great Migration', occurring over a period of roughly a dozen years from 1630 until the outbreak of Civil War in England temporarily ended emigration in 1642 (Godbeer 1992: 2). By 1638, Puritan colonists in New England numbered around eight thousand (Winship 2005: 1). It is these newly founded Puritan communities in New England that serve as the setting for *The Witch*, and with which we'll concern ourselves for the rest of this section.

PURITANS IN NEW ENGLAND

A group of Puritans, convinced that God was preparing to remove his favor from England, left for the colonies in November of 1620, landing in Massachusetts in December. While this group was given the name 'Pilgrims' much later on, it was not a name they claimed for themselves – they were part of the Puritan movement (Winship 2018: 72). They gradually established a colony at Salem, and John Winthrop was named the first governor in 1629, while Winthrop was still residing in England. The following year, he led a group of eleven vessels, carrying nearly a thousand Puritans, eager to settle this new land (Or, at least a land that was new to the Europeans). These settlers viewed their mission as not one primarily rooted in socio-economic factors, but divinely ordained. As Allen Carden writes, 'Winthrop and his followers believed that it was God's work they were doing and that they had received a commission from the Lord himself for the establishment of godly English society on the shores of Massachusetts Bay in New England' (1990: 29). It was not the individual's responsibility to behave as a godly man himself: the goal was to create an entire society that existed in righteousness, under God's grace.

A page from John Winthrop's journal

Before leaving for New England, John Winthrop delivered a lecture entitled 'A Model of Christian Charity', in which he employed the phrase 'City on a Hill' to describe the society the Pilgrims hoped to create, paraphrasing Jesus's words from the Sermon on the Mount in Matthew 5:14.[3] In the popular imagination, this phrase is meant to invoke the hope that the Puritan's city will be a visible symbol of virtue, that the force of the Puritan's goodness will inspire others towards godliness. This is the sense in which John F. Kennedy famously invoked the phrase in his 1961 speech. However, it's not quite the sense that Winthrop had in mind. Rather than seeing the Puritan settlement as a positive example for others to follow, Winthrop imagined that the visibility of the Puritans' plan of creating a virtuous, godly society would set them on a pedestal such that the world would be watching if they failed (Gaustad and Schmidt 2002: 52-53). The Massachusetts Bay Colony would be a city upon a hill, the pastor continued, 'So that if we shall deal falsely with our God in this work we have undertaken and so cause him to withdraw his present help from us, we shall be made a story and a byword through the world.' Their experiment was audacious enough that the price of failure would be high: they would be a disappointment to God, and an object of mockery for the world. It was a high stakes game they were playing, and they felt the pressure all the time.

It wasn't long after the establishment of the colony that trouble came to the city on the hill, in the form of several controversies that divided the community. Each of these controversies is a relevant piece of the backstory to *The Witch*.

ANNE HUTCHINSON AND THE ANTINOMIAN CONTROVERSY

The antinomian controversy centered around one of the most famous of Puritan women, Anne Hutchinson. Hutchinson is still admired for her refusal to bend to the colony's religious authorities, and the great wit and eloquence she employed in holding fast to her views.[4] In a context in which women were not encouraged to take leadership roles, Hutchinson stood out for her boldness and her unflinching confidence in the face of a patriarchal authority system that was arrayed against her.

Hutchinson had visions which she believed were direct revelations from the divine, and argued that these revelations – whether they came to her or anyone else, provided they were true visions from God – were of higher import than any church doctrine. Because these revelations were the highest form of religious authority, Hutchinson saw no need for pastors or other leaders in the church. It's not hard to imagine why the authorities of the Massachusetts Bay Colony didn't like this too much. Puritan court records indicate that this controversy, and Hutchinson's subsequent trial and banishment, occurred primarily from the years 1636-1638.

Hutchinson arrived in Massachusetts Bay in 1634, along with her husband and eight of their children. Hutchinson had been feeling increasingly unhappy with the direction of the Church of England, a feeling that was confirmed by a vision she had around 1630 which revealed to her that England was destined for destruction (Winship 2005: 16-17). After her arrival in the colony, she continued to challenge the religious authorities. Her religious views on issues such as salvation were not in accordance with Puritan doctrine. But perhaps even more troubling from the perspective of the colony's religious authorities was her habit of holding house meetings, during which she preached to a growing number of followers (Godbeer 1992: 4).

Hutchinson's fame has endured over almost four centuries largely on account of the speeches she gave at her trial.[5] The judges gave her multiple opportunities to disavow her beliefs and promise to stop preaching her unorthodox views, all of which she refused. The trial resulted in her banishment from the colony.

Much of what angered the Puritan establishment about Hutchinson's views was her assertion that most of the Puritan ministers (with the exception of John Cotton, in whom she found an ally for a time) were preaching a false gospel; she charged them with preaching a 'covenant of works' (LaPlante 2004: 51), a charge which cuts to the very heart of the Protestant Reformation. As we have seen above, the Puritan anxiety over salvation loomed large, as it does over The Witch's family, so it was not uncommon for Puritan ministers strongly imply that salvation could be guaranteed through obedience. While the obedient man could not be assured of salvation, this outward obedience was at least one sign of salvation, according to a common refrain of Puritan homiletics. Hutchinson would have none of this, instead arguing that 'good or bad conduct is irrelevant in determining who is saved' (Pagnattaro 2001: 10). For Hutchinson, looking to outward behavior to attempt to interpret the will of God was akin to blasphemy, indicating a deep lack of trust in the divine will. Rather than being an attack on the fundamental beliefs of Puritanism, Hutchinson's views 'took Puritanism to its farthest reaches' (LaPlante: 2004, 54), since Puritan doctrine itself agreed that salvation was granted through grace alone. Hutchinson didn't want to overturn Puritan doctrines; she wanted to hold Puritans (especially ministers) to account for the logical conclusions of these doctrines.

Furthermore, Hutchinson believed that ministers were not needed as interpreters of doctrine, since the individual believer could be directly connected to Christ. Hutchinson believed she had received these revelations directly from God, frequently while reading Scripture, and that the Holy Spirit had also granted her the gift of prophecy; as such, there was no need for herself, or any other believer, to rely on ministers as intermediaries. For Hutchinson, it was this direct connection with God and Christ that mattered, not the approval of the religious leaders. In the 19th century, these views came to be known as 'antinomianism', literally 'against the law', because they saw no outside authority as being higher than the revelation granted to an individual believer.

Hutchinson defended these views in the trial's public forum forcefully and unapologetically. Eventually, John Cotton, her ally in the pulpit, abandoned the cause and recanted his views, so Hutchinson stood alone to defend herself (Pagnattaro 2001: 4). In contrast to John Cotton, Hutchinson held firm to her religious convictions, and her persistence resulted in her and her family's banishment from the colony. In the spring of 1638, Hutchinson left to join other exiles from Massachusetts in a nascent colony in New Hampshire, settling there for several years before moving to New Netherlands, now near New York City (Pagnattaro 2001: 44-45). The Wecqueasgeek tribe raided the settlement in 1643, killing Hutchinson and the three families who remained with her (Winship 2005: 145-146).

To this day, Hutchinson remains a symbol of integrity, and a powerful example of a woman who stood her ground in the midst of a patriarchal system that was designed to silence women like her. Her influence is seen most strongly in the opening trial scene of *The Witch*, when William refuses to bow to the Puritan tribunal, resulting in his banishment from the colony. As with Hutchinson, it is easy to admire his firm convictions; but for both William and Hutchinson, these convictions came at a steep cost.

NEW ENGLAND WITCH TRIALS

Over four hundred years later, the Salem witch trials remain one of the defining episodes of American history. They have come to stand as a cautionary tale against the idea of American exceptionalism, a warning that self-righteousness can have calamitous results for entire communities. When the American political scene was roiled by Joseph McCarthy's HUAC (House Unamerican Activities Committee) hearings in the 1950s, in which anyone who had ever had an association with leftist causes was asked to come before the committee and name the names of their fellow travelers, playwright Arthur Miller responded by writing *The Crucible* (1953), a devastating dramatic interpretation of the Salem witch trials. While the connections are clear, Miller made them even more explicit in his autobiographical writings. Miller writes of the HUAC hearings, 'The main point of the hearings, precisely as in seventeenth century Salem, was that the accused make public confession, damn his confederates as well as his Devil master' (quoted in Bigsby 2003, x). For Miller, Salem is a symbol of righteous crusades run amuck, warped and twisted by a group's blind certainty that they alone possess the truth. In more modern times, the circle has turned around again: the term 'witch hunt' is now frequently used by a variety of public figures facing scrutiny. By employing the 'witch hunt' language, the accused seek to deflect legitimate charges and lump them in with the witch hunting hysteria of Salem. In recent years, it's become a staple of Donald Trump's tweets, a shorthand for him to claim complete innocence of wrong-doing, while at the same time claiming his opponents have lost sight of reason.

The events that transpired in Salem of 1692 are well-known; however, because the reasons behind them have proven so inscrutable, they have been subjected to endless analysis. They have been preserved in the trial records of the colony, and letters and papers from many of the key figures have survived as well.[6] Much of the following narration comes from these preserved documents, as well as scholars who have spent much of their career pouring over them.

Actor Lionel Stander testifying before HUAC's witch hunt

The events emanated from Salem Village, located a few miles outside of the Town itself (Ray 2015: 15). Salem Village was designated a Parish in 1672, which allowed it to call its own minister but stopped short of granting the Village full autonomy. This was only one of the pressures that the community of Salem Village was experiencing. In recent years, there had been increasing conflicts with the indigenous tribes of the region, including an attack which destroyed the town of Falmouth in 1676 (Ray 2015: 53). One of the main accusers of witches was Mercy Lewis, a young maidservant from Thomas Putnam's house; her family had fled from Falmouth after this attack. For many, the attacks of the Native Americans were of the same provenance as witches – both were sent from the Devil, in an attempt to tear down a shining light of the kingdom of God. Many of these attacks were part of the escalating conflict between French and British settlers, which came to be known as King William's War (1688-1697). Raids on New England settlements were increasingly common during these years, placing the Puritan communities even more on edge than they might have otherwise been.

The religious life of Salem Village was not immune from these tensions. The Village developed the reputation of chasing its ministers out of town, largely under the agitation of the wealthy Putnam family. Part of this might be due to Salem Town's refusal to allow the ministers of Salem Village to be fully ordained – they were allowed to preach, but not given full rights to oversee the sacraments. It was into this tense situation that Rev. Samuel Parris was called as Salem Village's minister in November of 1689; with Parris's calling, Salem Town relented and allowed for his full ordination, authorizing him to administer baptism and communion (Ray 2015: 16). Prior to Parris's ordination, for the Village residents to receive these sacraments they had to make the journey into the town proper.

Samuel Parris's ministry proved controversial from the start, as he used his pulpit to draw sharp lines between those families in the Village who were full members of his church and those who maintained membership in churches of surrounding towns and villages. Less than a year after Parris's ordination, a Village meeting authorized a tax-rate committee, which voted to withhold the funds for Rev. Parris's salary (Ray 2015: 24). (His salary was funded completely by the non-voluntary taxation of the Village citizens, regardless if they were members or not of Parris' church.) This divide between the members of Parris's church and non-members grew wider, inflamed by Parris's rhetoric during his sermons. Church attendance in Salem was compulsory for all, so these sermons were events for the entire village. Unless families wanted to trek several miles to a neighboring church, they were stuck listening to Rev. Parris castigate them.

It's against this backdrop that things started to get strange within the Parris household. In January 1692, nine-year-old Betty Parris began experiencing violent seizures, throwing herself around the house uncontrollably. Young Betty was soon joined in these symptoms by her eleven-year-old cousin Abigail Williams. Rev. Parris was quick to blame these disturbances on evil forces, bent on undoing his good work in Salem Village. With influential Boston preacher Cotton Matther's recent text on witchcraft, *Memorable Providences*, in mind, Rev. Parris called in Dr. William Griggs to evaluate the girls in February of 1692. Witchcraft was the diagnosis.

Neighbour Mary Sibley suspected that supernatural evil was the root of the problem, and took matters into her own hands. She convinced two of the Parris household slaves, Tituba and John Indian, to bake a 'witch cake' of rye flour, mixed with the girls' urine. This unappetizing concoction was then fed to the Parris family dog in some attempt to counteract the black magic, but the reasons are a little murky. As Stacy Schiff hypothesizes, it could have been intended to work 'by drawing the witch to the animal, by transferring the spell to it, or by scalding the witch' (2015: 26), but whatever the specifics it was clearly an attempt to catch the party who was responsible for bewitching these girls. When this attempt was brought to light, Reverend Parris railed against Mary Sibley during his Sunday morning sermon, arguing that this misguided attempt to drive out the Devil had only invited him closer.

While this conflict was simmering within the community, another group of young girls began experiencing these same symptoms, and blamed Tituba and several other of the village women of using witchcraft against them. Judge Hathorne sprung into action, aggressively questioning Tituba until she 'confessed', spinning elaborate and fanciful stories of her contacts with the Devil. Transcripts of Hathorne's questioning have been preserved; it is easy to imagine why a slave woman would tell this frightening figure anything she thought he wanted to hear. Tituba became the first suspect to spin a story of her encounters with the Devil and offer the names of other supposed witches in the Village; from there, the witch hunt was on.

Over the next few months, Salem's courthouse was the hottest ticket in town. Some suspects were questioned by the judges in private, certainly with strong coercion if not outright torture. And when the suspects were brought into court, the accusing girls served as the star witnesses for the prosecution. They acted out their maladies on command, frequently claiming that one of the suspected witches had placed a spell on them at that very moment. 'Spectral evidence' was deemed to be admissible by the Salem court, meaning that anything the girls claimed to have seen, which was hidden from the eyes of others by supernatural means, could be entered as evidence against a supposed witch. So the girls continued to report on visits they received in the night, even from people who were locked away in jail awaiting trial. Sometimes, they even saw ghostly visions of witchcraft during the trial.

The trials went on for most of 1692, spreading to neighbouring communities. Andover, in particular, was hit hard by an epidemic of witches – of the town's six hundred residents, fifty were accused of witchcraft. The trials finally came to an end in October when the governor of Massachusetts ordered the Court to disband. Boston intellectuals had become increasingly concerned with the trials' impact on public order, and had started to view them as an embarrassment to the colony. A few scattered trials continued in various nearby communities in the early months of 1693, but ended with a whimper. In all, nineteen people were executed for witchcraft (five of them men), along with two dogs. Most of these deaths were by hanging, though Giles Corey was killed by 'pressing', a horrifying method which involved slowly placing more and more stones on top of him until he was eventually crushed to death. The slow methodical method of execution was an attempt to draw out a confession, but Corey did not yield. Five additional suspects died in jail awaiting trial, due to the poor conditions of the Salem Town jailhouse. Scholar Benjamin Ray tallies '152 arrests, 54 confessions, 28 convictions' (2015: 1) in the Massachusetts Bay Colony in 1692. But the fever broke as swiftly as it arrived.

The motives of the young women at the epicenter of these accusations has remained one of American history's greatest mysteries. Medical causes such as hysteria have been proposed, and even rotting food causing a hallucinogenic effect has been suggested as a culprit. More sociologically inclined researchers have suspected that the power dynamics of Puritan society played a large role in the girls' theatrical performances – here, finally, was a space in which they were allowed to have some control over their lives, and to exert some authority over others. While all of these ideas are intriguing in their own right, we're left with nothing but tantalizing clues, and no hope of reaching a certain conclusion.

The only judge to publicly apologize for his role in the witch trials was Samuel Sewall, who recanted in a speech read before South Church of Boston in 1697 (Francis 2005; Sewall's apology is reprinted on pp. 181-182). In subsequent years, many of the jurors expressed regret, believing they had been mistaken in their verdicts. Gradually, the Massachusetts colony cleared the names of those who had been convicted, in some cases offering compensation to surviving families (Ray 2015: 156). While most of the witch hunt's victims were given exoneration by the early part of the 18th century, the last group of victims was only officially declared innocent by the State in 2001.

Besides the obvious connection with witchcraft, *The Witch* makes use of many of the anxieties that served as the backdrop for these trials. The vulnerability of Salem Town in the face of French and Native American attacks finds a parallel in the family's isolated farmstead. At several points in the film, Jonas and Mercy play the part of the Salem girls in the courthouse, enacting their attacks by writhing around on the floor and claiming Thomasin is at fault. And the family's suspicion of one another, so quick to jump to charges of witchcraft as a response to difficulties and familial tension, could have come directly from the court records of Salem, 1692.

RELIGION, WITCHES, AND THE WITCH

Even on a first screening, most viewers pick up on the centrality of religion to the horror of *The Witch*. The family that we follow out of Salem and into the woods is a deeply pious family, led by the strong faith of their patriarch. He leads them in prayer on multiple occasions, serves as religious instructor for his son, and wrestles with his own inner demons in explicitly religious terms. And at every point, this religion is deeply embued with the Calvinistic faith of the Puritans.

Each of them, in their own way, expresses anxiety about whether they will be able to live up to the strict standards set forth by their religious tradition. Each of them is deeply afraid of falling short of these expectations, and each of them also harbors resentment for what their faith asks them to give up. By the end of the film, the pressures have grown too great, and their anxieties explode in eruptions of rage. While their faith was meant to be what allowed them to endure through difficult times, it instead ends up being a key element of their downfall.

When the book returns to provide a fuller reading of each of the film's characters, this religious background will play an extremely important part. In order to provide an even richer picture, it is important to situate *The Witch* in its generic context, with a particular eye towards exploring how it participates in the folk horror tradition.

FOOTNOTES

1. For the curious, these theses can be found in many places on-line, or in printed form in Bettenson and Maunder 2011: 197-203.
2. More detailed accounts of these events can be found in standard church history textbooks. In my own teaching, I have used Gonzalez 2010, as well as Dowley 2018: 307-352.
3. In the 1599 English translation known as the Geneva Bible, which is probably the translation Winthrop would have used, Matthew 5:14 reads: 'Ye are the light of the world. A city that is set on an hill, cannot be hid.'
4. Pagnataro, 2001 places Hutchinson in the context of American women who used oratory and literature to defy unjust laws, including Harriet Beecher Stowe and Toni Morrison.
5. A compelling retelling of this trial, based on the written accounts, can be found in LaPlante 2004: 11-18, 39-49.
6. A brief summary of the events is found in Reynolds 2008: 52-59; a thorough academic treatment, making extensive use of the archival documents, is Ray 2015. A more accessible, yet still highly knowledgeable, account is Schiff 2015. The archival documents themselves have been published in Rosenthal 2009, and are also available online at the Salem Witch Trials Documentary Archive, housed by the University of Virginia (http://salem.lib.virginia.edu).

THE WITCH'S GENERIC, LITERARY AND FILMIC BACKGROUND

QUESTIONS OF GENRE AND WORLDVIEW

While the question of genre can be helpful in categorizing a film, genre in film and literature is even more useful as a tool for interpretation. In this section, we'll be exploring the genre of *The Witch*, arguing that it participates in arthouse horror and family horror but fits most productively with films in the folk horror category. While a somewhat nebulous and fluid category, folk horror allows us to make the most evocative connections between *The Witch*, other films within this generic category, as well as with the genre's still developing filmic conventions.

In earlier studies of genre, the primary concern was with taxonomy: how can a (somewhat arbitrarily determined) group of texts be said to participate in a set of ideas, such that they occupy a similar space within the literary world (Frow 2015: 55-60)? In this pursuit, of prime interest is the features inherent to any genre: for example, the *film noir* consists of detective stories, with a morally compromised protagonist, who encounters a *femme fatale* in the course of his investigation (Silver 1996: 3-15). The settings are primarily in the American city, and the films feature a stylized *chiaroscuro* cinematography, heavily indebted to German Expressionism. From this list of features, we can determine which films are included and which are not, based on the number of these characteristics they possess. So we can clearly see that *Double Indemnity* (1944) fits the bill, as does the 1946 version of *The Killers*. But what about *Out of the Past* (1947), with its rural setting, or *Ride the Pink Horse* (1947), set in Mexico? Or films like *Gilda* (1946) (or even *Mildred Pierce* [1945]) in which the style is clearly *noir*-infused, but the plot contains more elements of melodrama than of detective fiction? Is there a set amount of the characteristics on the list that a film needs to have before it can be included? And are some features more important than others?

However, it can't be the case, or at least it shouldn't, that all these categories do is help us to determine whether we're watching a horror film, a superhero action movie, or a romantic comedy. As viewers, we intuitively know what we're watching, and we understand how it participates in a wide variety of conventions. Whether a movie is a *film noir* with elements of a melodrama or a melodrama with *noir*-ish characteristics, or some other combination of parts of different genres, viewers are able to make these connections not because of a mental checklist of elements, but because of their experience with the genres represented.

Two major theories of genre attempt to circumvent this problem of the 'checklist'. In the 'prototype' theory of genre, each viewer holds in their mind a master template for each genre. We might think of *Halloween*, for example, as the slasher *par excellence*; when considering whether other films also participate in the genre of the slasher, we'd hold them up against *Halloween* in our mind, and see if they share enough features in common. This process is more slippery than it might appear at first – as viewers, we can't always articulate which film or work of literature we're using as the prototype. In fact, it might not even be a singular work at all, but an amalgamation of several works that we've blended together. And since there's no real police to determine whether a film is an acceptable prototype or not, each viewer is left with a wide range of possibilities for determining what fits within a given genre. It is up to an individual viewer, and the scholars, to determine whether *Halloween* is the best prototype for the slasher genre, or whether *Friday the 13th* (or *Psycho*, or *Peeping Tom*) is more emblematic.

Another theory attempts to offer more flexibility in a somewhat different manner. Taking a cue from Wittgenstein's ruminations on what constitutes a 'game' (Wittgenstein 1958: 31-32), Fowler uses the model of 'family resemblance' to talk about genre. For Fowler, we don't have rigid checklists of features that we're looking for in genres, but we have mental groupings of things that seem to go together in one way or another (Fowler 1982: 41-42). If our minds perceive a family resemblance between, say, *Halloween* and *Friday the 13th*, we can understand both films as slashers. Depending on how we interpret and experience the film, we might lump *Psycho* into this category as well, since we perceive it to be of a similar type.

While determining whether a film or work of literature is 'in' or 'out' of a genre can be a fun parlor game, genre can offer more than this simple categorization tool. More interesting from a perspective of both viewership and scholarship is what generic categories *do*. Genres help us to read and experience film and literature. Generic frameworks help us to understand a work on its own terms, while at the same time helping to moderate conversations between works.

Russian linguist and literary theorist Mikhail Bakhtin famously argued that genres were not tools for categorization as much as windows into a worldview.[1] As much as dictating plot points or character arcs, genres construct moral worlds, with each new entry into a genre participating in the growth and development of the genre's characteristics. Some genres are very clear in the worldview they attempt to convey: we might think of fairy tales, in which straying from the path can lead to dangerous consequences, which the child hero must overcome before being reunited with their family. Or the slasher film, in which sexual activity and other transgressive behavior inevitably leads to death. Or the *film noir*, in which all the characters are morally compromised, and trying to look out for themselves in a morally compromised world, but are unable to escape their own past.

Thinking of genres in terms of worldviews opens up a host of interpretive possibilities. We can start by thinking about not only about whether or not, and to what degree, a particular film participates in a given genre. But we can also think about what the participation in a genre signifies, which elements of the genre are emphasized for which specific purpose, which elements have been left out and why, and how the film's participation contributes to the film's worldview and overall meaning. We can see how the genre has shaped the contours of the film, but also how the film has contributed to the genre, offering generative possibilities for conversations with both subsequent films and previously existing members of the genre. The idea of genres as worldviews can help us to move away from thinking of genres as fixed categories, and instead look at them as tools for understanding how a particular film is constructing its moral world.[2]

THE GENRE OF *THE WITCH*

The Witch has been grouped together with the so-called 'Arthouse horror' films of the 2010's, such as *It Follows* (2014), *The Babadook* (2015), *It Comes at Night* (2016), *Get Out* (2017), *Hereditary* (2018), *Suspiria* (2018), *Us* (2019), *Midsommar* (2019) and Eggers' second feature film, *The Lighthouse* (2019).[3] In some ways, these films sit together uneasily. They don't share much in terms of structure, setting, or pacing. They may be very slow-paced (*The Witch, Midsommar*) or move briskly (*It Follows, Get Out, Us*); they may be quite restrained in their use of gore (*The Babadook*, *The Witch*, *It Follows*) or feature graphic set pieces (*Hereditary*, *Suspiria*, *Midsommar*). But they share enough in tone and style that critics (and marketing departments) have felt comfortable in lumping them together.

One thing these art-house horror films do have in common is the focus on subtext. All of these films lend themselves quite readily to academic analysis, and articles have started to appear on most of them; those too new to have been given the academic treatment are sure to have their turn shortly. *The Babadook* has been read as concerning 'trauma suppression in the domestic sphere' (Pheasant-Kelly, 2019), while *It Follows* has been discussed as an update on the slasher film, with a shift in focus towards the trauma of adolescent sexuality (Barbera, 2019). And of course, the scholarship on *Get Out* has become its own industry, with articles and volumes on *Us* sure to follow (Lloyd, 2019, is one excellent example).

While the settings and elements of monstrosity are highly varied within these films, the above-mentioned films all participate in the mode of family horror; while the terror may sometimes come from without (as in *The Witch*, *It Follows*, and *It Comes at Night* in particular), the fear also emanates from within the family itself. This has been the subtext of numerous horror films, particularly since the late 1960's (with 1959's *Peeping Tom* and 1960's *Psycho* as early forerunners).

Film critic Robin Wood, in his seminal essay 'The American Nightmare', argued for the year 1968 as the beginning of the modern era of horror, with the twin release of *Night of the Living Dead* and *Rosemary's Baby* (Wood 2003: 63-84). For Wood, the sharpest contrast comes from an examination of where the films locate the source of horror. In contrast with the horror films of the 1930's and '40's, and the science-fiction/horror films of the '50's, horror was a threat from without. Dracula was a foreign immigrant, the Mummy was born of ancient Egyptian mythology, and aliens or communists were encroaching on our national borders. But in the late 1960's, films began exploring the idea that horror was a natural outgrowth of patriarchal family structures. Earlier films such as *The Bad Seed* (1956), *Peeping Tom* and *Psycho* had introduced this idea previously, but Wood argues that it became the dominant mode of horror starting with *Rosemary's Baby* in 1968.[4] By the time the 1970's rolled around, horror was well-versed in the horrors of the family, in films such as Wes Craven's *The Last House on the Left* (1971, and even more starkly in 1977's *The Hills Have Eyes*) and Tobe Hooper's *The Texas Chainsaw Massacre* (1974).

But as is apparent in this list of representative family-horror films, the category seems too broad to be categorized as a genre; along with *The Witch* and *It Comes at Night*, we could also include David Gordon Greene's *Halloween* (2018) re-boot, in spite of its stark differences in tone, plot structure, and methods of characterization, in the category of family-horror. This leads to the conclusion that family-horror is more constructively thought of as a mode than as a genre; an important theme that can be found across a number of genres, but too broad to constitute a genre in itself.

So in which genre does *The Witch* most comfortably lie? The following section will make the case that the most comfortable (and meaningful) home for *The Witch* is within the genre of folk horror.

FOLK HORROR

Folk horror is more easily discussed under the 'family resemblance' concept of genre discussed above than it is analyzed by a strict set of guidelines. The films and works of literature that fall under the umbrella of folk horror are easily identified as sharing some things in common, but a singular, all-encompassing definition has proven elusive.

In his monograph on folk horror, Adam Scovell identifies director Piers Haggard's 2003 interview with Fangoria magazine as the origin of the term (Scovell 2017: 7). While struggling to reach a definition, and enjoying the play that the term's ambiguity allows, Scovell describes folk horror as being the space 'where the re-appropriation of past culture, even that which is still within living memory, now attains a folkloric guise and becomes ascribed as Folk Horror' (Scovell 2017: 7).

There's a bit of a circularity to this definition, but it's nonetheless an effective starting point. Folk horror is that strand of horror in which the pre-modern, still present in the form of oral tales, escapes the clutches of the campfire tale and walks among us. While the settings are often rural, recent decades have seen more and more folk horror tales that find the pre-modern still living in the city. However, even in these narratives, it's

Horrible folk of The Wicker Man *(Robin Hardy, 1974 © British Lion)*

often the case that urban folk horror is a remnant of the city's pre-industrial past; a film like *Candyman* (1992) is a perfect example of this (Towlson 2019: 33-36). In short, folk horror has taken the stuff of folk tales, often already fairly horrific in their own right, and re-purposed them as horror movies, novels, or short stories. Folk horror is horror, with folklore as its backbone.

Frequently, the landscape is a highly salient feature. In folk horror, the protagonist is usually in an environment which is not natural to them, an environment which becomes unsettling or even threatening. Karra Shimabukuro has referred to this as the attitude of 'marveling' which characters take towards the environment (frequently the forest) in folk tales; for her, it is this attitude of marvel that most directly connects contemporary works of folk horror (in the specific case she is referring to, the original television series of *Twin Peaks*) with the broader folkloric tradition (Shimabukuro: 2016, 121). In folk tales and works inspired by them (Shimabukuro cites Shakespeare's *A Midsummer Night's Dream* as an example), 'the forest is often dark, the source of evil, and sometimes knowledge' (*ibid.*). This attitude towards the environment, viewing it as both the source of threat and wonder, is one of the key elements that binds many works of folk horror together.

Towlson has argued that another key element which distinguishes folk horror is its emphasis on storytelling, the focus on the horror film as a story that is being told. In this manner, Towlson distinguishes *Candyman*, with its focus on the nature of urban legends, from films such as *Halloween*, which may take the *form* of an urban legend but which do not reflect on the nature of storytelling themselves (Towlson 2019: 36). In this sense, we might see John Carpenter's *The Fog*, with its opening scene invoking the campfire tale, as participating in folk horror – we might even make a similar decision regarding *Urban Legend*, as it frames its murders as oral folktales come to life. Folk tales are passed down through generations by the act of oral transmission, by storytelling. Likewise, films that fall under the umbrella of folk horror frequently situate themselves as participating, in one way or another, in this oral tradition.

We've now identified three major elements of folk horror: 1) events centred on the (often pre-industrial) past; 2) an environment which invokes both wonder and dread, in audience and characters; and 3) the element of orality is foregrounded in the narrative itself. Having established this (far from complete!) set of characteristics, we will briefly discuss some of the important milestones in folk horror to see how they interact with the tradition and each other, then seek to place *The Witch* within this tradition.

FOLK HORROR IN THE BRITISH TRADITION

While folk horror can be located within many cultural traditions, this necessarily brief overview will focus on the folk horror tradition in Great Britain, followed by its American counterpart. While some have argued that America lacks a folk horror tradition, this section will argue strongly in favor of a tradition of American folk horror that is distinct from the British tradition. It is within this tradition of New England folk horror that *The Witch* can be most usefully situated.

The British folk horror tradition is usually thought to emanate from three films produced in the late '60s – early '70s: *Witchfinder General*, *The Wicker Man*, and *Blood on Satan's Claws*.[5] All three share a bucolic environment which seems to become an integral part of the plot and an emphasis on practices that are thought to have been left behind with the modern era. The self-conscious emphasis on story-telling is lacking in these three films; this seems to have been a later development in the folk horror tradition.

These three films are, in some ways, quite different, with *The Wicker Man* being set in modern times, *Blood on Satan's Claw* including verifiable elements of the supernatural, and *Witchfinder General* having more of the structure of a picaresque. In Ian Cooper's 2011 Devil's Advocates monograph, written before the term 'folk horror' had entered into academia, Cooper identifies *Witchfinder* most closely with the Western tradition, arguing that the British countryside becomes the equivalent of Ford's Monument Valley as the setting for a tale of masculine pride and morality (Cooper 2011: 57-62). Nonetheless, there's enough of a family resemblance between these three films that scholars have frequently tried to group them together.

Vincent Price in the bucolic landscape of Witchfinder General *(Michael Reeves, 1968 © Tigon)*

Scovell argues for a shared lineage based on some common factors: 1) landscape, 2) isolation, 3) skewed belief systems of morality, and 4) the happening/summoning (Scovell 2017: 17-18). Scovell suggests that this last item is the 'weakest link in the theory to argue' (Scovell 2017: 18), and that it really boils down to the inevitable climax of the narrative, to which the other items have been inexorably leading. *The Witch* seems almost to have been created with this list of characteristics in mind, as it clearly checks off every box.

The British folk horror tradition has remained strong, with more recent entries such as *Hollow* (2011) and *Wake Wood* (2009) continuing the genre's emphasis on the ancient powers that linger into the modern world, mostly dormant but occasionally awakened to wreak havoc. In *Hollow*, a monastery in the Suffolk countryside is haunted by pre-Christian forces; the found-footage format participates in a new form of orality, as the

film's supposed pre-existence as home movie foregrounds the idea of storytelling.
(Much in the manner of American folk horror film *The Blair Witch Project*, on which see
below.) In *Wake Wood*, a family loses their young daughter to a dog attack, but learns of
a way to bring her back for three days to say their goodbyes. *Wake Wood* focuses more
on the ritualistic elements often present in folk horror, as well as the common thread of
a dark mysticism that lurks beneath the rational surface of the modern world.

THE AMERICAN FOLK HORROR TRADITION

We might more accurately say 'Traditions' in the plural, as American film and literature
has several regional varieties of folk horror. There is folk horror about the West, such
as *Grim Prairie Tales* (1990), *Dead Birds* (2006), *The Burrowers* (2008), and, perhaps most
famously, *Ravenous* (1999). There is Southern folk horror, such as *Two Thousand Maniacs*
(1964), *Skeleton Key* (2005), or the unfortunately titled *The Haunting in Connecticut 2:
Ghosts of Georgia* (2013). You might even include *Texas Chainsaw Massacre* (1974) in this
list as Texas folk horror, particularly in the way the film's protagonists find themselves in
conflict with the older generation's obsolete ways of living. There are also folk horror
films with urban settings, such as *Candyman* (1992) and *Urban Legend* (1998). But the
American variety of folk horror with the longest lineage, and perhaps the greatest
influence, is that which emerged out of Puritan New England.[6]

We can see the earliest beginnings of folk horror in the folktales of New England
themselves, stories passed down through oral tradition that take the form of cautionary
tales, encounters with the supernatural, and other tales of the weird and eerie. Moritz
Jagendorf's collection of re-told New England folk tales includes a handful that he traces
back to Massachusetts, including one entitled 'The Devil in the Steeple'.[7] Jagendorf begins
the tale thusly: 'This happened when no place in all America was so much troubled by
the Evil one as the State of Massachusetts, the state of the Pilgrim Fathers. Truly there
was no city or hamlet there that didn't have some kind of trouble with the devil' (1948:
153). Already, we see a key element of Puritan religion creeping into the folktale: the
Massachusetts Bay Colony was to be a city on the hill, a shining example of moral purity
for all to see; because of this, it drew special attention from the Devil. Rooted in the
Puritan worldview, this strand of folk horror, centered on the presence of witches and

devils, spread to other parts of New England as well. Jagendorf's collection reflects this, with devilish tales from New Hampshire, Rhode Island, and Vermont, as well as tales of witches he gathered from Maine and Connecticut. In the literary canon, these tales greatly influenced 19th century New England fiction, particularly the work of Nathaniel Hawthorne.[8]

Nathaniel Hawthorne had Salem in his blood; his great-grandfather was Judge John Hathorne, known colloquially as the 'witch judge' for his central role in sentencing more than 150 men and women to prison, and another twenty or so to death by hanging or torture (Reynolds 2008: 51). Hawthorne's lineage also included a great-great-grandfather who had been a driving force behind the persecution of the Quakers in the Massachusetts Bay colony. Hawthorne writes about both of these men in his preface to his most well-known work, *The Scarlet Letter*. Opining that he does not know whether or not these ancestors have repented of their persecuting sins in the afterlife, Hawthorne remarks, 'At all events, I, the present writer, as their representative, hereby take shame upon myself for their sakes, and pray that any curse incurred by them…may be now and henceforth removed' (Hawthorne 2014: 10; originally published 1850).

Hawthorne may have tried to exorcise these ancestors from himself, but the ghosts of Salem haunt much of his work. In *The Scarlet Letter* and a number of this short stories, Hawthorne distills the Salem Witch trials down to two lessons, both of which Hawthorne believes reveal fundamental truths about humanity: 1) When people use extreme means in an attempt to make things better, they will always make things worse; and 2) These efforts to create a perfect society, and the fixation on human perfection that these efforts entail, leave people bitter and distrustful of their fellow humans. (Historian Larry Reynolds has argued that these two impulses were also behind Hawthorne's distrust of the abolitionist movement, in spite of his dislike of slavery; Reynolds, 2008). These two propositions are explored clearly in a pair of Hawthorne's short stories, both of which provide interesting conversation partners to *The Witch*.

Hawthorne believed the Puritans to have been (mostly) sincere in their beliefs, but too caught up in their own certainty and righteousness to realize the consequences of their witch hunts. Hawthorne reflects this directly in his short story 'Earth's Holocaust', which imagines a giant bonfire in which the people of the world throw all of the material goods and symbols that have prevented them from building a perfect society, including money, family crests, and other signs of prestige. As the last bottle of liquor is thrown into the fire, a small group of men laments the loss of all the pleasure in the world. The world has perhaps become a safer, more just place, but has also been drained of all its joy. However, they take consolation in the words of a 'dark-complexioned personage', who assures them that they 'shall see good days yet', for the fire did not consume 'the human heart' (Hawthorne 2011: 330; originally published 1844). In their zeal to throw all of life's evil into the fire, the story's reformers have left the world a drab, dreary place. More than that, their efforts will prove unsuccessful, since the human heart remains the source of the world's evils, not the symbolic and material items that have been burned.

Hawthorne's early story 'Young Goodman Brown' (written in 1835) presents a Salem resident who stumbles upon a witch's Sabbath during a nighttime walk. The tale contains many of the folkloric elements that have been associated with the devil and witchcraft, including a gentlemanly Satan who carries a staff that seems to 'twist and wriggle itself like a living serpent' (Hawthorne 2011: 195). (And, as Scovell has noted as a characteristic of folk horror, the forest becomes a living, menacing character of its own.) While they walk together, Satan gives a brief overview of some of the ways he has been involved in the history of Salem, including the Puritans' persecution of the Quakers and their burning of Native American villages. Their walk takes them deeper into the woods, where Goodman Brown recognizes his neighbors, including his wife Faith, all worshipping the Devil. When Goodman renounces Satan, the scene disappears, and he is left wondering whether it was an actual encounter with the Devil or only a dream.[9] Nevertheless, Goodman cannot shake the feeling that all of his neighbors are secretly in league with the Evil One and lives out the rest of his life a bitter man, estranged from his community and his wife. For Hawthorne, this is the cost of the Puritan fixation on the morality of one's neighbor. In the case of Goodman, it leaves him distrustful and miserable. In *The Witch*, this same distrust leads to the breaking apart of the family. 'Young Goodman Brown' has clearly left an influence on modern American horror; Stephen King has described his short story 'The Man in the Black Suit' as an 'homage' to Hawthorne's tale (Cowan 2018: 28-29).

FOLK HORROR CINEMA IN THE NEW ENGLAND TRADITION

While these folkloric tales continued to be written in New England, the folk horror tradition developed in film as well. Perhaps the earliest example of New England influenced proto-folk horror in cinema is from William Dieterle's 1941 film *The Devil and Daniel Webster*, based on a short story from Stephen Vincent Benét. From the opening shot, the film situates itself as a folktale – a title screen tells the viewers: 'It's a story they tell in the border country, where Massachusetts joins Vermont and New Hampshire. It happened, so they say, a long time ago. But it could happen anytime – anywhere – to anybody…' (Jabez's farm is located in 'Cross Corners, New Hampshire', but the film's spirit is Puritan through and through.) We are not so much watching a movie as listening in on a campfire tale, one that just happens to have been filmed.

The Devil and Daniel Webster – Old Scratch comes to New England (William Dieterle, 1941 © RKO)

The film follows the tale of hard-luck farmer Jabez Stone, who faces the prospect of losing his farm to a greedy loan shark. As the film opens, Stone suffers a series of misfortunes – his pig escapes as he is heading out to church, and in trying to recapture the animal he falls in the mud and spoils his Sunday clothes, breaking the pig's leg in the process; while trying to take his calf and seed to his creditor, the wagon flips over, knocking Stone's wife to the ground; then, while gathering the seed to sell, the bag catches on a protruding nail in the barn, spilling the entire contents into a mud puddle. At this point, Jabez calls out that he'd gladly sell his soul to the devil for good luck; in response, who should appear but 'Old Scratch' (played with delicious relish by Walter Huston, father of John and grandfather of Anjelica – the only family with three generations of Academy Award winners). Jabez agrees to sign his soul over to the devil for seven years of good luck, starting immediately with a bag of gold that miraculously appears under the floorboards of his barn.

From very early on in the film, the contours of the plot are set in motion – Jabez Stone's clock is set to seven years, marked by a date which Old Scratch carves into a tree to remind Stone (and the viewers) when his time will be up. In this, we see the inevitable conclusion that Adam Scovell discusses as a key element of folk horror. The landscape, while less important than in subsequent folk horror films, also plays a key role in the film. In the early scenes, the mud of the Stone farm is a constant presence, ruining Jabez's church clothes and the seeds he hoped to sell at the market. And the gnarled tree, standing as a reminder of the contract Jabez has signed, is a presence the camera returns to with frequency, a reminder of Jabez's folly and his impending fate.

As the time draws near for Jabez to fulfill his contract, he calls on Daniel Webster for aid, the best lawyer in the land. Webster challenges Old Scratch to defend his contract in court; the Devil agrees, and hastily summons a jury of Benedict Arnold and other notorious American outlaws and traitors, with none other than Judge Hathorne presiding. Undaunted by this motley crew, Webster nonetheless wins the case, arguing that Jabez's soul was not his to sell, thus voiding the contract. The film ends with Old Scratch, beaten but not defeated, looking in his book for a new name to visit, before turning his eyes directly into the camera and fixing his grin on the viewer.

This film contains the elements that Scovell identifies as constituting the folk horror chain, though one is in modified form. As mentioned above, the importance of the landscape is established in the opening shot of Old Scratch looking out over the Stone family farm. Scovell's next requirement is isolation. While this element is not as strong in *The Devil and Daniel Webster*, we still see it in the way that Jabez continually pushes people away from him as he grows more and more comfortable with the worldly goods that have been bestowed upon him; this motif reaches its climax when Jabez throws himself a housewarming party for his new mansion, and none of the townsfolk show up. Scovell's third point is that of 'skewed values', in which the moral systems of the past (and usually, by extension, of the present) are called into question. *The Devil and Daniel Webster* fulfills this through its focus on the corruption Jabez's character undergoes. At first, he only wants enough money to stave off foreclosure on his farm. But soon, we witness him transforming into a predatory creditor in his own right, taking advantage of farmers who are in the same position Jabez was only a short time ago. And in case this message wasn't clear enough, we also learn that Jabez's former creditor, the stingy (and uncomfortably Jewish-coded) Miser Stevens, has also signed his own contract with Old Scratch. Scovell's element of the summoning is fulfilled when Daniel Webster and Old Scratch finally confront one another in a battle of courtroom wits. It is the climactic summoning that the narrative has been creeping inexorably toward since the beginning.

In addition to these elements, the film foregrounds itself as being rooted in oral tradition, 'a story they tell in the border country'. This is not a story made up out of whole cloth, the film announces, but one that has been told by the people, long before this film we're about to watch came about. It is a folk tale, re-imagined as a Hollywood film. Other films have followed in its wake, drawing on these folkloric elements while more explicitly framing themselves as horror. In several other examples, including *The Witch*, we'll see these elements from *The Devil and Daniel Webster* repeated, and recombined into new forms.

FOLK- MEETS FOUND-FOOTAGE HORROR: THE BLAIR WITCH PROJECT

Since the turn of the millennium, the cultural impact of horror films has been at one of its historical highpoints. Horror has often seen ebbs and flows, including highpoints such as the 1930s (Skal, 2001) or the 1970s (Wood, 2003). After these highpoints have subsided, there are periods where horror films enter a period of relative quiet, when horror movies don't regularly become a part of the mainstream conversation. The 90's were one of these low points, with horror films struggling to make much of an impact in either the box office or among critics. Two films released near the end of the decade changed that, ushering in the wave of box-office horror successes that continues to the present: M. Night Shyamalan's *The Sixth Sense* (1999) and Daniel Myrick and Eduardo

Sanchez's *The Blair Witch Project* (1999). While *The Sixth Sense* can be viewed as an important predecessor for its re-introduction into mainstream cinema of restrained, slowly building horror, emphasizing characterization and atmosphere more than jump scares or gore, a more direct connection to *The Witch* can be made with *The Blair Witch Project*.

The folkloric forest of The Blair Witch Project *(Daniel Myrick, Eduardo Sánchez, 1999 © Haxan Films)*

It's hard to overstate the influence of *The Blair Witch Project* (hereafter *BWP*) on contemporary horror films. With its simple plot outline, location shooting, and 'found footage' conceit, it launched a horde of micro-budget, DIY imitators, a wave which coincided with the rise of Netflix and other distribution methods which were less reliant on major studios.[10] *BWP* demonstrated that a small group of committed cinephiles, armed with little more than a digital camera and a great idea, could make a believable, affecting horror film in a short amount of time, on a budget that could barely afford a shoestring. By situating itself as 'found footage', with the supposed 'actual' video taken by the characters in the film, the obvious low budget quality and flaws became part of the film's structure. This simple formula would be emulated by (relatively) big-budget studio productions like *Cloverfield* (2008), *The Last Exorcism* (2010), and *Chernobyl Diaries* (2012). And there were many similar projects that started off as small-budget affairs, only to find major distribution after receiving buzz on the festival circuit, such as *Paranormal Activity* (2007). One could also add to this list the number of small-budget films such as *[Rec]* (2007) or *Grave Encounters* (2012) that found a strong cult audience outside of traditional distribution channels, along with dozens of imitators that showed up on streaming services or in Wal-Mart's bargain DVD bins.

What set *BWP* apart from its many imitators was its grounding in the traditions of folk horror. It features all of Scovell's major markers of folk horror, again with varying degrees of prominence. Perhaps most notable for *BWP* is the use of nature as a character; by the end of the film, the woods have become a living, menacing presence. In a haunting scene, the characters ford a river, then note that they already crossed this river yesterday, even though they've been travelling in a straight line away from it ever since. For the characters, this is evidence that they are lost and have been wandering around in circles, but the viewers know better. The forest is a living, hostile presence, in league with the Blair witch, and the characters have been caught in a loop in which traditional markers of time and space no longer hold. The forest also serves as a continual reminder of the characters' isolation, as they are unable to escape from its clutches. The film culminates in a form of Scovell's 'summoning', when Heather and Mike find the house in the middle of the woods, which we can instantly sense is not a friendly place. Famously, Heather finds the missing Josh in the house's basement, standing in a corner in a way that recalls one of the townspeople's descriptions of a local serial killer's method. While the witch is never seen, her presence is finally made known in this concluding scene. Scovell's element of 'skewed values' is present only tangentially in this film; the characters, operating from a modern worldview, follow in the long line of horror-film protagonists who do not heed the wisdom of the townsfolk, and instead believe they will be able to debunk the legends and rumors of the witch who haunts the forest. Their modern conception of reality is not able to conceive of the supernatural evil that exists in the woods, and this inability to consider the limits of their worldview is their undoing.

While participating in these elements of folk horror, *BWP* foregrounds the element of the folk tale as told story in a unique method: through its status as found-footage. With the film's initial screen announcing this film as being edited together from the footage of the main characters, *BWP* situates itself explicitly as a film whose story has a life outside of the film. This is not simply a movie, the producers would have us believe; it is a story with a long history prior to the film, and a story that will continue after the film is over. It is, in short, a folk tale.

This illusion was aided by the pseudo-documentary 'The Curse of the Blair Witch', which first aired on the Sci-Fi network before the film's release and was subsequently included as an extra feature on most DVD and Blu-Ray versions of the film. While portraying itself as an exploration of the legends surrounding the Blair Witch, including mock interviews with actors portraying themselves as townspeople and scholars, the film was actually a work of fiction, created by the filmmakers of *BWP* as an elaborate marketing tool. It helped *BWP* achieve its intended effect, as many filmgoers were convinced of the film's veracity (Wenzel, 2019).

Telling a campfire tale in The Fog *(John Carpenter, 1980 © AVCO Embassy)*

A similar feature, though much less elaborately staged, was present in *The Devil and Daniel Webster*, in which the opening intertitle declares the film to be a story told throughout New England. Similarly, John Carpenter's folklore-tinged film *The Fog* (1980) begins with a group of children listening to the story behind the fog's legend around a campfire. *The Witch* participates in this tradition simply and elegantly with its subtitle: *A New England Folktale*. Unlike their British counterparts, these New England versions of folk horror are consistently explicit in their foregrounding of their status as folk horror. Each example makes a clear attempt to link itself to New England myths, legends, and folk tales, by announcing itself as emerging from these traditions.

THE WITCH AS FOLK HORROR

The Witch participates in this trajectory of folk horror, perhaps even more deeply than the examples listed above. It leans heavily on all the elements Scovell identifies as forming the folk horror chain, is explicitly rooted in the folkloric traditions of New England, and grounds itself as a tale being told through its subtitle. These elements are not merely tangential details which happen to be present in *The Witch*, but are all central to the film's narrative.

From the family's first arrival at the location of their homestead, the landscape is a central feature. After their expulsion from the colony, the family travels consist of brief scenes of their leaving the settlement on a rickety horse-drawn cart, then camping overnight in a forest, before finally arriving in the clearing they will make their home for the remainder of the film. Their homestead rests on a flat, grassy plain, large enough for farming and grazing, but small enough that they are always reminded of the forest that looms over them. As they first arrive at this clearing, the family kneels together on the ground, offering their thanks to God, but the camera pans upwards to the forest. This is the presence which will always be with them. As the Puritans envisioned themselves as occupying a 'city on a hill', surrounded by the world on all sides and constantly exposed to its evils, so is the family a vulnerable group, beset by this forest all around them. Frequently, a new scene will begin with an establishing shot of the homestead, filmed with a moving camera from the vantage point of the forest. Often, twigs and blades of grass move in and out of the camera's way. While these are never identified as POV shots, they clearly give the impression of some unknown entity watching the family from the edge of the forest. Most likely, something that is malevolent.

The forest continues as a motif throughout the film. After the family has established their homestead, Thomasin takes young Samuel from Katherine. As Thomasin walks away holding Samuel, a soft drumbeat emphasizes a quick cut to the woods. This shot of the woods holds for several seconds, with an ominous minor-key chord droning softly in the background. Thomasin's 'boo!' affords the opportunity for another cut, this time to the smiling face of Samuel, lying on his back as his big sister plays peek-a-boo with him. But after several rounds of this game, Thomasin opens her eyes to find Samuel gone, his empty blanket lying on the ground. The camera pans up from this empty blanket to the woods, remaining still as Thomasin yells, 'Samuel!' and runs towards the forest. But she stops short, unable to enter.

However, Eggers' camera has no such hesitancy, leaving Thomasin at the edge of the woods but entering itself. As the audience, we are privileged to follow the witch into the woods and witness the disturbing ritual to which she subjects poor Samuel (though lighting and editing makes it difficult to tell exactly what is happening). The forest is hence marked as a space that is dangerous for the characters, one which intrudes upon the domestic sphere, and which is associated with danger and the occult. Throughout the film, the woods return as a lingering reminder of this unsafeness, a looming presence that persistently encroaches upon the family's homestead.

Thomasin at the threshold (© A24)

On two occasions, the family (William and Caleb in particular) view the woods as a necessary danger, entering it for the purposes of hunting and trapping. While they understand the danger that the woods represent, they also have an urgent need for food, and the woods represent a possible source. In both instances, the incursion into the woods results in tragedy rather than sustenance. Furthermore, these two expeditions into the woods are undertaken through deceit; when William takes Caleb into the woods, it is on the condition that they do not tell Katherine where they have been. Upon their return, Caleb invents a lie to explain their absence. Seeming to have learned well from his father, Caleb later undertakes to sneak out at night, hoping to return with food before his parents are aware of where he has gone. Both incidents result not only in physical danger for the characters involved, but in damaged relationships and a further erosion of trust among the family.

Aside from a brief shot of the family camping as they are searching for a suitable location for their homestead, the family's first trip into the woods is when William takes Caleb on a hunting expedition. While aiming at a hare, his gun misfires and the family's dog is lost when it chases after the fleeing (and mysteriously ominous) animal. And later, when Caleb enters the woods with his sister, the two of them are separated and Caleb meets the witch in her most seductive form, leading directly to Caleb's ultimate demise. The woods are always present, and always menacing.

The woods also serve to emphasize Scovell's second element of the folk-horror chain, that of isolation. From the film's beginning, isolation is a key motif. In the initial trial scene, we see the family standing alone, with the judges looming in front of them and the disapproving townspeople behind. This isolation is further emphasized when the family leaves the settlement. A POV shot, revealed to belong to Thomasin, watches the residents of the settlement walking through the streets, pausing briefly to look before going about their business. Then, with little fanfare, the settlement's wooden door is closed behind them, and they are on their own. The family's isolation will play an increasingly important role in their disintegration, a theme which will be explored further in the 'Close Reading' section.

Scovell's third element, 'skewed belief systems of morality', is evidenced throughout the film. The family's Puritan belief system is a driving force behind all of their characters, and is reflected in almost all of their interactions with one another. But this belief system is also shown to require expectations which are impossible to achieve, damaging to all involved, and ultimately destructive for the family unit. William's righteous certainty drives the family into the isolation of their homestead, and Thomasin's prayers reveal a deep-seated anxiety over whether she is good enough. These elements will all be explored more fully in the sections on each individual character, as well as in the 'Close Reading' section.

And finally, the film moves inexorably towards Black Phillip's appearance as Satan; a more literal representation of Scovell's category of 'summoning' could hardly be imagined. The evil that the family has feared throughout the film finally becomes known in the flesh, and Thomasin's final decision becomes inevitable. (Or perhaps revealed as inevitable, as it had been all along.)

In the next section, we will move into an overview of some of the film's folkloric elements, before exploring the conflicts and arcs of each character in depth, including each member of the family and Black Phillip. With the background of *The Witch* as folk horror established, this section will make clear that each member of the family participates in the unbreakable 'folk horror chain' that Scovell has described, leading the film to its inevitable conclusion.

FOOTNOTES

1. Bakhtin can be a frustratingly unsystematic thinker, making the search for clear definitions in his work difficult. However, a good place to start with his thinking on genre is the essay 'Epic and Novel: Towards a Methodology for the Study of the Novel,' in Bakhtin 1981: 3-41.
2. A different approach to film genre in particular is found in the influential work of Altman, 1999, who argues that genres are inherently stable, and the process of their growth and development involves a continuous accumulation of sub-genres.
3. For a discussion of art-house horror, see, for example, Ebiri 2014; Zinoman 2018.
4. Tony Williams's *Hearths of Darkness* still remains the most thorough examination of the family in horror films; the second edition provides an even more detailed reading of this theme.
5. These three films, and their influence on the development of folk horror as a generic category, are discussed in Scovell 2017: 11-34.
6. Edward Ingebretsen (1996) has argued extensively for a Puritan influence on American horror in general, drawing a direct line from Cotton Mathers to Robert Frost, then to H. P. Lovecraft and Stephen King. While some of his arguments might seem forced, the monograph makes many intriguing connections.
7. Jagendorf 1948: 153-157.
8. Other colonies have their own overlapping yet distinct folk horror traditions; perhaps the most well-known adapter of such tales is Washington Irving, whose famous tales 'Rip Van Winkle' and 'The Legend of Sleepy Hollow' draw on the traditions of the Hudson Valley. An excellent introduction to the Hudson Valley ghost story tradition, including Irving's work, is Richardson: 2003. For an academic exploration of the Puritan religious influence on the American horror tradition more broadly, see Ingebretsen, 1996.
9. Reynolds 2008: 68-69, argues that Hawthorne connects 'Young Goodman Brown' to the Salem witch trials through the idea of spectral evidence, evidence of a dream-like quality

which caused Goodman to distrust his neighbors for the rest of his life and, in the case of the Salem witch trials, caused people to be falsely accused and executed for witchcraft.

10. *The Blair Witch Project* wasn't the first horror film to utilize the found footage conceit; this honor is usually given to the 1980 Italian film *Cannibal Holocaust*. But *BWP*'s enormous success was what started the found footage trend.

FOLKLORIC ELEMENTS IN *THE WITCH*

In addition to its foundation in Puritan religious beliefs, *The Witch* relies heavily upon folkloric elements.[1] Many of these elements are European in nature, representing folk tales that stem from both the British Isles and continental Europe. Even though the film is set in the 1630s, very soon after the family would have immigrated to the colonies, the folk traditions in the colonies quickly emerged as highly distinct from those in England or Continental Europe. So Eggers takes some creative license, borrowing influences from various European traditions, and from some New England traditions which seem somewhat later than the time period of *The Witch*. Some of these would likely be familiar to a Puritan family in 1630s New England, while others would more likely be unknown. Even so, this mix of folkloric elements contributes to the detailed atmosphere of the film, which most viewers find to be both completely foreign and utterly believable. After all, for the characters of *The Witch* the events of the film aren't rooted in folklore – they're rooted in the malevolent attacks of the witch of the woods, and the devil who is orchestrating all of the events.

THE DEVIL WEARS BLACK

While the Devil only appears briefly in *The Witch* (at least in human form), his presence hovers over the whole film. For his portrayal of the Devil, Eggers leans heavily on Puritan ideas and imagery, which developed out of the European tradition of the Middle Ages and the Reformation. Of course, the Devil could be addressed in the section on Puritan religious beliefs; he is included here because Eggers' portrayal of him is rooted less in the doctrines of religious institutions than in folk tales and other popular conceptions of the Devil. Even so, the Devil is only one example of the extremely blurred line between religious beliefs and folk tales; often, one cannot be distinguished from the other.

Many people are surprised to find that the Devil doesn't appear very much in the Bible, particularly in the Old Testament, and that when he does appear he's not really the guy with a red cape and horns that we've come to know. This image of the Devil comes from other sources – our conception of the Devil has much more to do with Milton's *Paradise Lost* (1667) or Dante's *Inferno* (1472) than with the Bible. It's quite a while

Lucifer being cast out of heaven, as imagined by Gustave Doré

before the Devil develops the persona of the dashing rebel, as portrayed by Milton, or the overlord of Hell, as depicted by Dante. Instead, in the Old Testament he's just another of the divine beings who works for the highest God, one whose role is to mete out punishment on the guilty.

For most of the time when the Old Testament was being written (roughly 1200 BCE – 160 BCE), the religious landscape of ancient Israel did not have a devil. God was responsible for both good and evil. While we often associate the devil with the serpent in the Garden of Eden, this isn't how the story in Genesis depicts things; the serpent is just a snake, albeit one who walks around and talks. It's not until later, in the New Testament book of Revelation (written about 100 CE) that the serpent of the Garden becomes associated with the Devil. (Or perhaps a little earlier, in a book included in the Roman Catholic Bible, but not the Bibles of Protestants, called 'The Wisdom of Solomon'.)

If you search through the Old Testament, you won't find the word 'devil' at all. You'll find 'satan' a few times, in the books of Job, Chronicles, and Zechariah. But most of the time when this description is used, 'satan' isn't a name, but a title – in Hebrew, the word means something like 'adversary', or perhaps 'executioner' (Stokes, 2019), and it often includes the definite article, 'the satan'. In book of Job, it's clear that the satan is in the employ of God, and his job includes serving as God's eyes and ears on the earth, seeing if there are any weak spots in God's creation that might need addressing. He causes trouble, but that's his role. Many scholars have compared him in this book to a sort of prosecuting attorney. When the Old Testament is translated into Greek, 'the satan' is translated as 'diabolos', meaning something like 'slanderer'. It's from 'diabolos' that we get our English word 'devil'.[2] In Ryan Stokes' comprehensive new monograph on the history of the Satan, he argues that the figure of a satan undergoes a gradual change prior to the dawn of Christianity, from one who exacts God's punishment on the guilty to one who attacks the innocent (Stokes, 2019).

The diabolos/devil appears much more frequently in the New Testament, though usually as an indirect reference rather than as an actual figure. Jesus makes a few references to a devil, who seems to stand in the way of God's plans, but Jesus only actually meets him once (although in a story that's told in three of the four Gospels, with very little variation). After Jesus is baptized, he wanders into the desert on a sort of vision quest. In all of the accounts, Jesus goes to the desert and 'is tempted by the Devil'. In these temptations, the Devil engages in conversation with Jesus, trying to trick him into a vain demonstration of his power, or into bowing down to worship the Devil. The Devil proves himself to be an excellent student of the Bible, quoting the Psalms and Isaiah in an effort to nudge Jesus away from his divine mission. These attempts prove futile, and the Devil gives up after three attempts, without further harassing Jesus. Katherine references this event in one of her bedroom conversations with William. When William mentions how God has protected them through much, Katherine responds, 'Was not Christ led into the wilderness to be ill met by the Devil?'

In this story from the Gospels, we see several aspects of the Devil that will prove important in the developing traditions of Satan, and in *The Witch*. The Devil is reserved, eloquent, and attempts to persuade rather than to overpower. The only power the Devil has is that which someone else gives to him. The Devil is not granted the power to directly, physically attack individuals – his only power is indirect. He does, however, have the ability to cause calamities around individuals in the hopes of causing their faith in God to waver. In an even more indirect manner, he has the power to plant feelings and ideas within a person, feelings and ideas which they can either accept or reject. And as *The Witch* demonstrates, he has the power to encourage false beliefs, breaking apart families through the power of distrust.

Gustave Doré, illustration for Paradise Lost *(1885)*

While the Devil's power is always indirect, in American folklore the Devil has been viewed as playing a number of different roles, shifting slightly through the course of history. W. Scott Poole has traced the different conceptions of the Devil's power in America, noting that this power changes from era to era: 'In the seventeenth century, Satan had been blighting crops and causing unnatural death through his pacts with witches. By the late eighteenth century, interfering with the work of the evangelical ministry had become his primary concern' (2009: 45). He attempted to accomplish these goals through frustrating plans, discouraging believers from attending revivals, or any other number of schemes which might seem more mischievous than evil. Poole notes that, through the nineteenth century, many American religious traditions gradually began to view the role of the Devil as shifting from attacking 'the individual soul' to being responsible for 'evil within the larger society', such as slavery or alcoholism (2009: 50-51). In all of these eras, the power of the Devil is indirect, and seeks to operate primarily through persuasion. If the Devil can place a seed of doubt in a believer, causing him to stay home rather than attend a revival, he's kept that soul from growing closer to God. And if the Devil strikes down a faithful family's crops, then perhaps that family will turn away from God in despair.

In the Puritan world of *The Witch*, the Devil is fixated on the soul of the individual. Whereas believers in the 19th century might believe that wrestling with the Devil was a necessary part of any Christian's spiritual formation, in Puritan New England an encounter with the Devil was, in itself, evidence of the believer's guilt (Poole 2009: 43). The Devil only appeared to the weak and vulnerable, whose faith was already wavering. Katherine shows evidence of a similar worldview in her reference to Jesus's being 'ill met' by the Devil in the wilderness. For the Puritan mindset, even Christ's encounter with the Devil was not an opportunity to overcome temptation, or part of life's struggles that the Christian might have to endure. Any encounter with the Devil indicated that a person had been abandoned by God.

The Devil played a major role in the Salem witch trials, and frequently appeared in the supposed confessions. In fact, the Devil was a central figure in the trial's very first confession, that of Rev. Parris's housemaid Tituba. In his questioning of Tituba, Judge Hathorne asked whether the Devil had asked her to sign her name in his book; after some prodding from Hathorne, she agreed that yes, the Devil had asked her to sign his book. Benjamin Rey suggests that this detail, first suggested to Tituba by Judge Hathorne, was 'modeled on the Puritan practice of making a covenant with God, which people signified when they became church members and their names were entered into the church record book' (Rey 2015: 39). Since the church's book was an important sign of the member's covenant with God and with each other, it seems reasonable that the Devil would have his own book, a mirror image of the one held in high esteem by the Puritan church. This detail would become important throughout the witch hunts of New England, as it provided suspected witches with an excuse for having seen the names of others in the village. Confessed witches could have recognized their neighbors at a witch's Sabbath, but they also could have seen their names in the Devil's book. The Devil's book also provides an important symbol at the climax of *The Witch*, as Black Phillip asks Thomasin to make her mark in his book, sealing their covenant.

The 15th century saw a rise in the belief that women were uniquely attracted to the Devil, a belief which historian Philip Almond attributes to Johannes Nider (Almond 2014: 101-102). This developing belief reached its apex in Dominican inquisitor Heinrich Kramer's notorious tract *Malleus Maleficarum* (*The Hammer of Witches*), a handbook for understanding and diagnosing the multiple ways that witches and the Devil were in league with one another. The next sections will offer a brief overview of developing ideas of witchcraft, leading to the understanding of witches held in 17th century New England.

BIBLICAL WITCHES

Like many of the concepts under discussion in this monograph, the presence of witches in the pages of scripture themselves is rather scant. While the germ of an idea is located in a few biblical passages, most of the religious conception of witches develops from the Church Fathers and later theologians.

Perhaps the most famous witch in the Hebrew Bible, the witch of Endor, isn't actually referred to as a witch at all. The Hebrew literally means 'master of the dead', which is why Esther Hamori prefers the title of 'necromancer' for her (Hamori, 2013; see also Grafius 2019a: 60-65). Outside of this one story about a witch who isn't a witch, there aren't any other stories about witches or witchcraft in the Bible. Perhaps the character most often associated with witchcraft, Jezebel the Queen, doesn't exhibit magical powers. She orders a group of prophets to be killed, and encourages her husband, King Ahab of Israel, to take a citizen's vineyard through eminent domain.[3] Only in a brief note, in 2 Kings 9:22, does a character make passing reference to Jezebel's 'sorceries'. As we'll see below, this is one of the words that sometimes gets translated as 'witchcraft', but this is really an anachronism; witchcraft, as we understand it today, hadn't yet developed as a concept. Still, the translation of the Geneva Bible, less scrupulous than many modern translations, would have identified many of these 'sorceries' as 'witchcraft', which would have been all that mattered to most Puritans.

For most of the references to witchcraft, one needs to turn to the legal material of the books of Exodus and Deuteronomy. But even here, there are only a handful of passages which reference the topic, and even these mentions are exceedingly brief. Frequently cited is Exodus 22:18; in both the King James Version and the Geneva Bible, the verse reads: 'Thou shalt not suffer a witch to live.'[4] The Hebrew word translated here as 'witch' is '*mekashephah*', literally a 'practitioner of sorcery', with a feminine ending. The reference is not to what became known as witchcraft, but to practices associated with non-

Israelite gods and goddesses, such as divination. The NRSV translates this same passage, more accurately, as 'You shall not permit a female sorcerer to live.' A similar prohibition is found in Deuteronomy 18:10, but here the participle is masculine in form. (Even in this form, the King James Version translates this word as 'witch', while the Geneva Bible uses 'sorcerer'.) Deuteronomy 18:10 also includes a prohibition against those who practice *qosem*, or soothsaying, which the Geneva Bible translates as 'witchcraft'.

While some of these passages have been interpreted as referring to witches, they really refer to religious practices that were outside of the Yahwistic worship of the time. It's only later that they will be applied to the developing idea of witchcraft. In order for this to happen, the church will need both a developed idea of the Devil (discussed above), as well as a history of hostility towards women. It is to this latter idea that we will now turn.

ORIGINAL SIN AND WOMEN IN THE EARLY CHURCH

We've examined the Puritan context that *The Witch* springs from directly, but this religious worldview has a long backstory in the history of Christianity. Of course, exploring this entire story is well outside of the realm of this monograph, but a brief tour through the development of Christianity's relationship between women, the Devil, and witchcraft provides some important contexts.

Today, many people are surprised to find that the phrase 'original sin' does not occur anywhere in the Bible. While later tradition blamed Eve for tempting Adam and causing the fall of mankind, this is an interpretation from later authors, perhaps most famously associated with Augustine in the late 4th century CE. If we read the text from the book of Genesis closely, it's clear that Adam was standing right next to Eve when she ate the apple, and she didn't do anything aside from hand it to him (Galambush 2018: 31). No tempting here.

But still, the idea that women are 'more credulous and therefore susceptible to demons', or 'more easily impressed than men by visions and delusions' (Almond, 2014: 101, summarizing the misogyny of Johannes Nidler) are fairly representative of the view of women throughout Christianity's history. Theologians and church leaders frequently viewed women as being associated with the physical and emotional aspects of life, as opposed to the 'masculine' realms of the spirit and the intellect. Since women could not be expected to control their emotions, they were easily misled. This meant that women were a prime target for the Devil's wiles, and as the concern over witches rose to a frenzy in early modern Europe, women found themselves the frequent target of witchcraft accusations. Indeed, recent studies confirm that somewhere between 70 and 80 percent of suspects put on trial for witchcraft were women (Rowlands, 2013: 449), frequently elderly widows who were considered unsociable or odd in some other way.

WITCHES IN EARLY MODERN EUROPE

Cover of a 1669 edition of Malleus Maleficarum, housed by the Wellcome Trust

Salem was far from the first outbreak of witch trials. Various writings from the 1430s describe witchcraft throughout Europe, including Germany, France, and Switzerland (Kieckhefer 2013: 160). Modern estimates place the number of prosecutions in Europe at around 90,000 (Robisheaux 2013: 179), most of which took place during the period of roughly 1400-1700. This period saw an increasing number of academic writings on witchcraft, most famously Heinrich Kramer's *Malleus Malificarum* (1487). Kramer's tome distilled and clarified much of the current European thinking regarding witchcraft, arguing for its basis in reality and its severe threat to the Church. Prior to this time, the Church's position had been that witchcraft was a heresy, but that people who thought themselves able to perform supernatural feats with diabolical assistance were actually suffering from delusions. But just a few years prior to the publication of the *Malificarum*, Pope Innocent VIII clarified the Church's perspective on witchcraft, moving to a declaration of its reality in the papal bull *Summis desiderantes*, issued in December of 1484. Walter Stephens describes the *Malleus Malificarum* and the papal bull *Summis desiderantes* as important milestones: '...one gave the most elaborate theoretical explanations, the other the most detailed papal condemnation of such crimes' (2003: 55). With some ebbs and flows, the Church would be extremely concerned with witchcraft in the coming centuries, leading to inquisitions, trials, and a variety of panics.

It is against this backdrop that the Puritans came to New England, bringing these anxieties and deeply held beliefs about the pervasiveness of witchcraft with them.

WITCHES IN THE COLONIES

As David Hall has documented in regards to New England, 'people were being punished for the crime of witchcraft long before the celebrated trials of Salem' (Hall 1999: 3). The presence of witches among their neighbors would have been a common anxiety for seventeenth century colonists, many of whom would have been quick to blame their neighbors for any misfortune that might befall their family, their livestock, or their crops. Witches could frequently be identified by the special teat, from which they gave suck to animals at night. (As is depicted in *The Witch* in Katherine's terrifying encounter with the raven.) Witches gathered in the forest to dance together, frequently naked in the active imagination of the male authority figures. And they had a menagerie of animals that gathered around them, helping to focus their magic and empower their wicked deeds. Many of these animals appear repeatedly in *The Witch*, scenes which become even more chilling once their resonance in 17th century beliefs regarding witchcraft has been explored.

ANIMALS

In *The Witch*, the presence of animals is usually ominous. Aside from the family dog, animals are either livestock or are associated with the presence of the witch. (Black Phillip is the major exception; he is a large enough presence in the film that he will be discussed along with the other characters, rather than with the animals.) In several places, the family's domestic livestock are afflicted with calamities, the particular nature of which have been associated with witchcraft in various accounts. In several instances, these incidents are associated with Thomasin. As William and Caleb are checking their traps in the woods, the scene is cross-cut with Thomasin finding a chicken egg which holds a miscarried foetus. And later, when Jonas and Mercy accuse Thomasin of witchcraft as she is milking a goat, the goat starts to produce blood. As Thomasin recoils from the blood, the camera cuts to a group of three faces in the barn, all staring at her accusingly: Jonas, Mercy, and Black Phillip. These events lead to further suspicion among the family members that Thomasin is already in league with the devil.

FAMILIARS AND SHAPE-SHIFTING

The hare and the crow occupy a different space, though the witchcraft folklore offers two possible readings of their role. Helen Parish notes that the British witch trials reveal that witches were thought to have animal companions, creatures which were connected to the witches' power and served as a sign of the witches' pact with the Devil (Parish: 2019). This was more common in Britain than in continental Europe. On the continent, witches were instead thought to have the power to shape-shift into animals (Rutkowski: 2019). Interpreting the hare as a familiar seems more likely; the raven is more ambiguous, and might be either a familiar or the witch in animal form.

A ruddy brown hare appears at several key junctures of the film, frequently standing motionless and staring directly at the characters. The hare appears twice when Caleb is in the woods – the first time with his father, as William and Caleb see it standing in front of them while they are hunting, and William raises his rifle to shoot it. Instead, the rifle misfires in William's face. More than simply being a portentous omen, the hare seems to have the power to make things go wrong for the witch's targets. In fact, In European folk

One of the witch's familiars (© A24)

culture the devil was often thought to appear in the form of a hare (Bever 2013: 57). In *The Witch*, there seems some ambiguity as to whether the hare represents the Devil or the witch's familiar; either way, it is a symbol of evil, and leads to bad things happening.

Caleb's second encounter with the hare, when he is with Thomasin, situates the hare as the witch's familiar. This scene strongly indicates that Eggers' choice of a hare was not accidental. Rutkowski recounts a tale found in a 16th century English pamphlet, which tells the story of a man on his way to work with his dog. A hare crosses their path, but instead of chasing it the dog whines and circles his master. The hare then departs and heads for the house of Mother Atkins, a suspected witch (2019: 25-26). This is particularly resonant with Caleb's second encounter with the hare, in which he follows it and is led straight to the witch's cottage. Just as in this 16th century pamphlet, the hare leads people to the witch's doorstep.

In the hare's final appearance, Thomasin goes out to the barn in response to some agitated noises coming from the sheep. She finds a hare, seemingly the same one that William and Caleb have encountered in the woods, sitting in front of the barn door as if awaiting her arrival. The presence of the hare in the barn might explain the various misfortunes Thomasin encounters there, including the goat whose milk turns to blood.

The raven appears only once in the film, though the scene is quite important. Kramer's

Malleus Maleficarum relates the story of a raven who travelled along with a witch to her execution (Parish 2019: 4). As will be discussed further below, Katherine sees both Caleb and Samuel after they have died. She takes Samuel in her arms and begins nursing him, and the camera leaves to follow the escalating fight between Thomasin and William. When the scene returns to Katherine, we find that she is not nursing Samuel, but is instead sitting in her rocking chair with a raven pecking at her breast. This is the point in the film where all hell breaks loose for the family. Until this point, they had at least some measure of security within the confines of their homestead, and particularly within the walls of their cottage. Here, the illusion of that security is shattered. Evil has definitively manifested itself inside the family's home.

FOLKLORIC RESONANCE

This backdrop is crucial for the effectiveness of *The Witch*. While sometimes borrowing elements that are more common to Continental Europe than to the Colonial setting, the deep connections to folklore still serve to create a world that seemingly lives and breathes. When combined with the religious background (which is, of course, hard to separate cleanly from the folkloric background), it creates a fully formed worldview within which to situate the characters.

It's to these characters, and the complicated relationships between them, that we'll now turn.

FOOTNOTES

1. See also the excellent work of Brendan C. Walsh (2020), which was unfortunately published too late to be used in this analysis.
2. I discuss this briefly in Grafius 2019a: 37-39 and endnotes; a much more thorough history is Stokes 2019.
3. Jezebel's story can be found primarily in 1 Kings 19 and 21.
4. The verse number is the verse number found in English Bibles; this verse is Exodus 22:17 in Hebrew. For a variety of reasons, there is sometimes a discrepancy in the verse numbering between English translations and the Hebrew. The verse numbers are not original to the text, however, and were added hundreds of years after the writing of the biblical texts.

CHARACTERS AND FAMILY DYNAMICS

As mentioned earlier, one of the film's most engaging elements is the relationships between the family members. Each of them exists within a complicated nexus, tied together with the other family members. However, each also has their own arc of character development, usually centered around an inner struggle which they are not able to overcome. This section will explore each of the characters in turn, then describe the series of relationships that drive the emotional content of the film.

WILLIAM

The family's dour-tempered patriarch, William is first seen standing resolutely before a Puritan court who has placed him on trial for heresy. He is a true Puritan head-of-household; in this trial, we hear him proclaiming that he cannot disavow his beliefs, for he believes them to be a true understanding of the Gospel. William's opening speech is perfectly in line with what we have seen from New England Puritan theology; he asks the judges, rhetorically, why all of the settlers have come to this land. William offers his own answer. It is not for the pursuit of freedom, as is often imagined of the Pilgrims, but 'for the pure and faithful dispensation of the Gospels, and the Kingdom of God'. William, like many of his fellow settlers, is not concerned with religions freedom, but with religious purity.

When one of the inquisitors tells William that holding firm in his conviction will result in his, and his family's, banishment from the settlement, William responds, 'I would be glad on it.' Even at this early juncture in the film, we see clearly that William holds his religious beliefs sacrosanct, placing them above the well-being of his family. As was discussed in the section on Puritan religion, this character trait is in keeping with the religious beliefs of the time; a man was responsible for not only his own salvation, but that of his entire household, and there was no more important task for a man than to maintain the spiritual purity of every member of his family.

William's extreme focus on matters of religion at the expense of his family's emotional life is highlighted throughout the film. After the infant Samuel has been kidnapped,

William instructs his son Caleb (© A24)

William has a conversation with Caleb, in which Caleb is concerned for Samuel's soul. 'Is Samuel in hell?' Caleb asks his father. Rather than giving words of comfort or consolation, William responds with a coldly Calvinistic theology: 'It is God above who knows who is Abraham's son and who is not.' There is no sympathy for a young boy's worry over his brother, simply the harsh calculation of double-predestination. Like Anne Hutchinson, William firmly believes that salvation is in the hands of God. Human worry about an individual's salvation is fruitless at best, and blasphemous at worst. William does little better in comforting the rest of the family in their loss: 'We must turn our thoughts to God, not to ourselves,' he tells them.

However, in other scenes he is not without compassion for his family. There are moments of tenderness between William and Katherine, as when the two of them are in bed together and they believe the children to be asleep. His pathos emerges most clearly in the wake of Caleb's death, when he does his best to comfort his grieving wife and daughter. While Katherine believes Caleb to have died in the throes of witchcraft, condemning his soul to damnation, William instead focuses on Caleb's final words of submission to Christ. Whereas William was unable to offer certainty regarding the fate of the infant Samuel, here he holds onto his hope that Caleb has achieved salvation. Katherine wails that he has been damned, that he let himself succumb to witchcraft. But William shoots back at her, 'He cried for Christ!'

William's tenderness similarly emerges shortly after in a moving scene with Thomasin. After Caleb expires, Thomasin runs outside in tears and William follows her. She collapses to the ground and William follows, embracing her. As he holds her, William tries to comfort her with hopeful images of the farm's future. He imagines how lovely the tree they are sitting under will be in the spring, and tells Thomasin of the wheat field he plans to plant nearby. It is one of the few times in the film that William is shown to find any joy at all in life, even if it is a forced joy in an attempt to console his grieving daughter. In this moment, William is able to be the steady patriarch that his family needs. This is one of the few times in the film when William, or any of the characters for that matter, are able to imagine a future with any hope. It's a hope that will not last for more than a few brief moments.

But these moments of compassion are few and far between for William. As the family's situation deteriorates, William struggles to hold his family together, and frequently does not live up to his own exhausting demands of perfection. We see this most clearly in the lies he tells to his wife, Katherine. Though always believing he is keeping the family's best interest at the forefront of his thoughts, William still has some troubles with honesty. He takes Caleb with him in the woods to check the traps, a dangerous place that the parents have agreed is off-limits to the children, then engages Caleb in a conspiracy to keep this fact from Katherine. And perhaps more damningly, William has sold the silver cup Katherine inherited from her father, but has kept this secret. When Katherine blames Thomasin for its disappearance, in spite of Thomasin's protests, William is only able to say, 'She says she hasn't touched it.' While he could exonerate his daughter from the charges Katherine lays against her, he instead chooses to remain silent.

William feels these burdens acutely, even if he is unable to express this mounting sense of frustration and his experiences of being overwhelmed by his responsibilities verbally. At several key junctures in the film, the tensions within the family build to a crescendo, and William responds by chopping firewood. As Aviva Briefel notes, William's wood-chopping seems 'a nod to the horror tradition', recalling both the father's wood-chopping in *The Amityville Horror* and Jack Torrance's obsessively repetitive writing in *The Shining* (2019: 8 n. 5). The first scene of wood-chopping occurs after William and Caleb have returned from their sojourn in the woods, and Katherine becomes angry that she is not being told the truth about where they have been. Frustrated at this challenge to his authority, he takes his frustrations out on the pile of logs. We next see him chopping wood as Caleb is lying in bed, unconscious and near death, after his encounter with the witch. In both instances, William's chopping wood is associated with a failed venture into the forest; first, when he and Caleb are unable to find any food in their traps, and the family squabbles upon their return; and second, when Caleb has been bewitched and is on the brink of death. Earlier in the film, William had told his son as they walked through the forest together, 'We will conquer the wilderness. It will not consume us.' William's wood-chopping is an attempt to will this statement into reality, a way for William to maintain mastery over the trees when it seems that he and his family have been defeated. The third and final time he is shown chopping wood is after Caleb has died, and William is left without his firstborn son as patriarchal heir. In this third scene, the full futility of William's wood-chopping is made clear. William sees Katherine lying in the grave, embracing Caleb's corpse, and looks on the futility of this gesture with pity. The scene immediately cuts to William's grunting, chopping more wood. The connection is clear: just as Katherine's attempt to bring her son back to life through her embrace is a pitiful act of futility, so is William's wood-chopping. He stops in the middle of his task, placing the axe down by his side, and laments, 'This is my fault.'

William's crisis is one of masculinity, and his inability to perform his role as patriarch. While believing himself duty-bound to leave the colony due to his firm religious convictions, William is unable to build a suitable homestead for his family. Through the course of the film, he watches as his children are taken, the crops fail, and his family is left with little prospect of survival on their own. William understands his sin as one of pride; near the end of the film, after locking his surviving children in the barn for the night, William prays alone in the rain (although he is observed by Thomasin through the slats of the barn in which she has been locked). 'I am infected with the filth of pride,' he confesses to God. 'Dispose of me how thou will't, but redeem my children.' His pleas will go unheeded. Even in this act of prayer and submission to God, William is unable to provide for his family in the way he so desperately wants.

Thomasin summarizes William's failures nicely in a vicious argument with her father, in which the restraint she has demonstrated throughout the film falls away. 'You let mother be as thy master,' she hurls at her father. 'You cannot bring the crops to yield. You cannot hunt. Thou canst do nothing save chop wood.' She attacks the elements that constitute

All work and no play… (© A24)

his masculine identity – his mastery of the household, and his ability to provide. But it is only after she mocks his wood-chopping that William explodes, knocking her to the ground and calling her a bitch (in one of the very, very few outbursts of profanity in the film). Even when his family was falling apart and he was unable to procure enough food, William could channel his frustration into wood-chopping. But Thomasin's insult reveals that this, too, is futile, and simply another expression of William's failure as a patriarch. In the end, Thomasin's insult proves prophetic. William meets his fate at the hand of the devilish Black Phillip; the evil goat gores William against the stack of firewood, the logs that William chopped in vain falling over his corpse.

THOMASIN

The film plays an interesting sleight-of-hand with Thomasin's character. William is the first character to speak, makes the decisions for the family, and is a dominant presence on-screen. Through years of film-watching, we've been primed to assume that, more likely than not, the family patriarch is the moral center of the film. It's easy to make the assumption that this is William's story. But by the end, it's become clear that Thomasin is the central protagonist. On subsequent viewings (or maybe on the first time through, for viewers more savvy than I am!), it also becomes apparent that the film leaves a trail of bread crumbs to lead us to this place, starting from the opening sequence.

While the first thing we hear in the film is William's voice, defending himself against charges of heresy before the colony's tribunal, the first shot is of Thomasin's face, passively observing. She is framed in a close-up, but looks upward, watching the judges, such that her eyes do not meet the camera. She is almost motionless as her father defends his beliefs. Next, the film cuts to a similar shot of Caleb, also watching the judges, then to Jonas and Mercy. Finally, we see William, but the camera presents us with the back of his head as he continues to speak, rather than his face. The back of William's head is in focus, with the judges blurred in the background. We might see this as a subtle way of increasing tension, by surveying the family and delaying the first appearance of the protagonist, then delaying yet again by filming him from the back. But when we see the back of William's head, we are adopting the viewpoint of his family; through this sequence of shots, we are led to understand that this film will not be about William as much as it will be about how his children experience him. After this sequence, the camera pulls back to a medium shot, showing the whole family from behind from the position of a spectator in the courtroom.

This all happens in tableau, with all of the observers motionless. A brief shot shows female spectators observing from one side of the courtroom, then male spectators on the other, before returning to the medium shot of the family from behind. It is during this shot that William refuses to recant, and the judge (still seen only in the blurry distance) delivers his verdict of banishment. As this statement concludes, there is a cut to a cross-section view of the family; this time, the camera presents them at a 45°angle, rather than the direct views we have been given until this point. It is also the first time we have seen multiple members of the family in the same frame together. (With the exception of Jonas and Mercy, who are treated more as a composite character.) Thomasin is in the foreground, followed by William, then Katherine, and finally William. William's face is shown here for the first time, though it is obscured both by the lack of deep focus and the brightly lit window next to which he stands. Most striking in this shot is that, for the first time, we see one of the characters move; Thomasin reacts to the verdict with a barely audible gasp and a sharp turn of the head towards her father, clearly expressing her disbelief that her father has allowed their situation to come to this. The rest of the family reacts passively (with the possible exception of Katherine, discussed below), but the sequence of shots highlights Thomasin's reaction.

As the family files out of the courthouse silently, Thomasin returns her eyes to the judges, and remains motionless for a moment, unable to process what has just transpired. It is not until Caleb calls her name that she turns and follows. While the dialogue has been between William and the judges, the gaze of the camera privileges the perspective and emotions of Thomasin. In this early scene, she is the only character to whose inner life we are granted access. William has the dramatic monologue, but the camera is subtly directing us to the starring role that will be played by Thomasin.

Thomasin tries her best to be a dutiful daughter, but her reaction to her father's steadfast refusal to renounce his beliefs is only the first time that we see this mask begin to slip. By the end of the film, it has fallen off completely. Not only does she realize that being the good daughter hasn't gotten her anything she wants out of life, but she has also realized that the expectations are impossible to fulfill.

After the family has left the colony and found the patch of ground on which they will homestead, the first action we are shown is Thomasin in prayer. This is also the first time we have heard Thomasin speak. This prayer reveals a young woman who has internalized her father's theology, believing herself to be deserving of 'all shame and misery in this life, and everlasting hell-fire'. The sins she confesses to seem minor, indeed, though they clearly loom large in the face of the Puritan anxiety which she has internalized. 'I here confess I've lived in sin,' she begins. 'I've been idle of my work, disobedient of my parents, neglectful of my prayer.' As the camera cuts to Katherine, nursing young Samuel, then a scene of William and the children harvesting corn, Thomasin's prayer continues

The dutiful daughter (© A24)

in voice-over. 'I have, in secret, played upon thy Sabbath, and broken every one of thy commandments in thought.' She continues, asking for God's forgiveness and mercy. Near the film's conclusion, we will see a sharp contrast between what she asks for in this prayer, and what the Devil understands her to truly desire in life.

We see her assuming multiple domestic roles, as she is frequently given responsibility for the younger children, washes William's clothes, and takes care of the animals on the farm. Through most of the film, she tries hard to be respectful of her parents, speaking as gently as possible when Katherine implies that Thomasin might have stolen her father's silver cup. (As discussed above, we later learn that Thomasin is innocent, and William chooses to offer her only a mild defense rather than reveal that he has, in fact, sold the cup.) For much of the film, Thomasin is the perfect Puritan daughter.

Even so, when things start to go wrong for the family, suspicion quickly falls on Thomasin. While New England witch trials more often featured young women as the accusers, with older women as the suspected witches, the landscape of horror is frequented with suspected, dangerous adolescent women. Viewers of contemporary horror films will no doubt recognize this trope from films such as *Carrie* (1976), *Ginger Snaps* (2000), and *Teeth* (2002), among many others.[1]

For the majority of the film, the viewer is only aware of two transgressions which Thomasin commits: taunting Mercy at the riverbank by assuming the persona of the witch, and sneaking off to the woods with her brother to check his traps. While Thomasin technically disobeys in this last action, it is with the intention of both protecting her brother and helping to provide food for the family. A more blameless daughter could hardly be imagined.

But as the family unravels, Thomasin's frustrations boil to the surface, and her mask of perfect daughter starts to slip. This is most prominent in her argument with her father, in which she (rightly) accuses him of failing in his duties as patriarch. In this conflict, her words are harsh, but from what has been presented of William's character they are all clearly true. Thomasin is far too honest to speak untruths, even in the heat of anger.

It is only after she has been falsely accused of witchcraft and her family lies dead around her that Thomasin signs her covenant with Black Phillip. This is not a decision made out of greed (as was the case with Jabez Stone) or an evil nature (as was suspected of the Salem witches), but out of desperation. Thomasin has been abandoned, left alone in the ruins of her family's homestead. She has nowhere else to turn. Just as she invoked the name of God in her earlier prayer, she here begins her speech by invoking the Devil. 'Black Phillip,' she says, 'I conjure thee to speak to me.'

While this invocation is an understandable act of desperation, we can also see that Thomasin has desires for a life with more tangible pleasures than the one she has. Thomasin has revealed a few hints of this throughout the film. As she is riding through the woods with Caleb, checking the traps for rabbits, the two of them remember their house in England, and Fowler lying in the sunlight. The detail the two of them can't agree upon is whether the windows had glass or not. Caleb is certain they did not; Thomasin is equally certain it did. 'Well,' Thomasin concludes, with a wistful smile, 'it was pretty.' While her spoken prayers are for forgiveness and mercy, these glimpses into her unspoken desires indicate a young woman who wants to be able to enjoy luxuries, even small ones.

When Black Phillip appears in human form, he responds to the unspoken desires of Thomasin's heart, which she tried unsuccessfully to deny in her prayers to God. When Phillip asks what she would like, her eyes light up with excitement. 'What canst thou give?' she asks. He responds with the desires of her heart: 'Wouldst thou like the taste of butter? A pretty dress?' And finally, in the quotation that launched a thousand memes, 'Wouldst thou like to live deliciously?' Black Phillip understands that what Thomasin truly wants is not purity or honesty, as she confessed to God, but physical pleasures and enjoyment in life. She wants the material goods that have been denied her in her family's struggle for survival. 'Yes,' she answers, breathlessly.

Eggers seems to have taken these details from historical accounts; in her (coerced) confession to the Salem court, Elizabeth Knapp claimed that the devil promised her 'money, silks, fine cloths, ease from labor, to show her the whole world' (Schiff 2015: 330). This last item is Black Phillip's final suggestion to Thomasin, an offer which she greets by calmly asking him what he requests of her. Only that she sign her name in his book, Phillip assures her, a detail that Eggers has also borrowed from accounts of the Salem witch trials. As was mentioned above, Rev. Parris's servant Tituba seems to have been the first witness goaded into confessing that she signed the devil's book; after her confession, this became a standard feature of confessions. Thomasin puts her mark in the book, then disrobes and walks into the woods to take her place in the witch's Sabbath.

As the conclusion of Thomasin's character arc is also the conclusion of the film, further discussion will be reserved until the reading of the film's conclusion, below.

CALEB

Like Thomasin, Caleb finds himself on the cusp of adulthood. He is being groomed by William to assume the role of family patriarch, and the film demonstrates him attempting to emulate William in other ways as well. As he accompanies William into the woods to check the animal traps, William leads him through a catechism, during which Caleb recites theologies of sin and the fallen state of man. He is clearly being raised to fill his father's shoes.

Caleb and William's foray into the forest, and the subsequent family drama that ensues when they return home, demonstrates another way in which Caleb idolizes his father and has learned from him. Caleb has learned that the patriarch has the right to lie, if he determines the lie is in the best interest of the family. When Katherine demands to know where they were Caleb is the one who speaks up, claiming that they were looking for apples. And not just any apples, apples like the ones they used to eat at home. He adds to this lie in a later scene, when he will be joined by Thomasin on his fatal late-night escapade into the forest. As William has taught him, he can deceive his family if the deception is in the service of taking care of them. Caleb has learned this lesson, and, as his lie about the apple demonstrates, has learned to do it well.

In addition to his emulation of his father, the other aspect of Caleb's masculinity which the film highlights is his sexuality. His burgeoning, and repressed, sexual desire is highlighted in several instances in which the camera provides a shot from Caleb's perspective of Thomasin's (extremely slight!) cleavage, a sight upon which Caleb lingers several times during the course of the film. During the first of these scenes, Caleb rises early as Thomasin is still sleeping. Through the POV shot, we see him linger on his sister's chest, then snap himself out of his brief revelry. But then he turns back for one last glance before pulling himself away. These shots find their rhyming echo in Caleb's encounter with the witch, who appears to him as a red-clad, beautiful woman, wearing a low-cut dress that offers Caleb much more cleavage than Thomasin. This temptation is too much for Caleb to withstand. Rather than looking away, as he does with Thomasin, he allows this woman to draw him in for what will prove to be a fatal kiss.

William scours the woods for Caleb and is unable to find him. The family have given him up for dead when Caleb stumbles back to the homestead, naked and barely alive. He falls into a sleep, and the family tries to go on with their work while they wait for him to wake. He awakens with a scream, and speaks a baffling, stream-of-consciousness blur of images, segueing into a deathbed prayer. The entire scene, all told, lasts close to ten minutes, over ten percent of the film's running time – a remarkable segment in this very tightly constructed film. A closer examination of Caleb's speech reveals dense series of quotations and allusions.

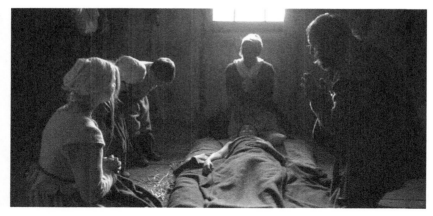

Caleb's deathbed (© A24)

An important textual reference is the court deposition of John Kelly, whose eight
year-old daughter, Elizabeth, died of a stomach disorder in Hartford, Connecticut, 1662.
Elizabeth was convinced that she had been bewitched by Goody Ayres. Caleb's first cry
is, 'Get the broad axe, he'll cut off her head! Get the narrow axe, he'll cut off her head!'
Caleb begins, statements which he repeats several times with increasing frenzy. In John
Kelly's deposition, he quotes his daughter as saying: 'Goody Ayres chokes me!' Elizabeth
called out. 'Father, set on the great furnace and scald her, get the broad axe and cut off
her head; if you cannot get a broad axe get the narrow axe and chop off her head!'
(Woodward, 2003). Similarly, Caleb still perceives himself as being tormented by the
witch, though the shift to the third-person in Caleb's cry is intriguing. This is no longer a
plea to the child's father, as with Kelly's statement. Instead, Caleb speaks with confidence
that his father will protect him. Eggers's has shifted from Kelly's plea for action to Caleb's
statement of certainty: if someone brings the axe to William, he will (definitely) dispatch
the witch. Unfortunately, all we've seen William cut with his axe in this film is a stack of
firewood.

Caleb gasps, and continues, 'She's upon me! She kneels! My bowels!' This also seems to
come from Elizabeth Kelly's dying speech. In Kelly's deposition, he recalls his daughter
saying, 'Father help me, help me! Goodwife Ayres is upon me! She chokes me, she kneels
on my belly, she will break my bowels, she pinches me, she will make me black and blue,

oh!' In a nod to New England's tradition, Eggers has lightly edited much of this speech and placed it into Caleb's mouth. After this outburst, Caleb's jaw clamps shut, and he momentarily goes silent.

Katherine holds him, while William uses the handle of his knife to pry open William's jaw. With his jaw open, Caleb is able to vomit forth blood, and a whole apple, with a single bit taken out of it to reveal a rotten core. Caleb most definitely succumbed to the temptation of the forbidden fruit.[2] Perhaps more importantly, this fruit was the subject of Caleb's lie earlier in the film, when he claimed the search for apples was the reason that he and William had been in the woods. Here, his lie has returned. And as Aviva Briefel points out, the apple didn't just serve as Caleb's lie, it was also a connection with the family's longed-for home in England. Briefel remarks: 'Caleb vomits out both his mother's and his sister's desires' (Briefel: 2019, 15).

Caleb is silent for a while as the drama shifts to the family attempting the Lord's Prayer (on which, see the section on Jonas and Mercy, below). When Caleb returns to the focal point of the scene, he reports on the various animals which the witch is using to attack him: 'A cat. A crow. A raven. A great black dog. A wolf,' all of which have been frequently attested as being familiars of witches.

Soon, however, Caleb cries out, 'My Lord! My Jesus!' and his lamentations turn to a prayer. This prayer, too, is the result of Eggers' research, with most of it being taken from a prayer recorded in Massachusetts Governor John Winthrop's diary. 'Kiss me with the kisses of thy mouth,' Caleb pleads, a passage taken almost verbatim from one of Winthrop's more famous prayers (Moore: 2005, 18-19). In another quotation from the same prayer, Caleb cries out, 'I am thine enemy, wallowing in the blood and filth of my sins.' This quotation helps us to read Caleb's deathbed experience. Some have wondered if Caleb's prayers are a mockery; Steve Wiggins, for example, suggests that 'Quoting Scripture here is a sign of bewitching…the boy has really been with a witch and was quoting the Bible out of context as a result' (Wiggins 2018: 119). While Wiggins's point is well-taken – the Devil himself can certainly quote Scripture, after all – I would argue that the allusions to Winthrop's diary points in a different direction. These lines from Winthrop indicate a devout believer, deeply conscious of his own failings, and trying to find his way back to God's grace. By employing these quotations, Eggers places Caleb in the same position. In Caleb's final moments, the invocation of Governor Winthrop's pious prayer indicates he believes he was heading towards that grace.

Caleb dies with this prayer on his lips, seeming to achieve an ecstatic vision in his last moments. Like Thomasin at the film's conclusion, he has transcended the restrictive structure of the Puritan family and found true joy, here in a connection with Christ. While this will be discussed further in the section on the film's conclusion, here it need only be noted that there are two characters whose screen time in *The Witch* concludes with overwhelming, transcendent happiness: Caleb, who finds this in a vision of God, and Thomasin, who finds it at the witches' Sabbath.

KATHERINE

For much of the film, Katherine works as hard as she can to fulfill the role of 'Good Wife', finding her primary identity in raising her children and pursuing domestic tasks, and supporting William in any way she can. Edmund Morgan describes the role Katherine plays perfectly in his description of the ideal Puritan wife. 'When she became a wife,' he writes, 'she gave up everything to her husband and devoted herself exclusively to managing his household' (1966: 42). The Puritan wife 'remained subject to her husband's authority', and 'was expected to depend entirely on his judgment' (1966: 43). Katherine dutifully tries to fulfill this role, but finds that trusting the judgment of her husband does not lead to a healthy and prosperous family.

Katherine's character is also described in the writings of Cotton Mather, one of the most renowned preachers of the 17th century. In his book *Ornaments for the Daughters of Zion*, published in the same year as the Salem witch trials, Mather describes his idea of the proper role and demeanor for women. A woman was to be modest, obedient, and above all, to 'maintain the fear of God'.[3] She should defer to her husband in all things, and to largely remain silent, her speaking 'as rare as silver' (Mather: 2000, 298). Similar statements can be found in numerous Puritan writings and sermons from 17th century New England.

In addition to being the Good Wife, Katherine also works to become the Good Mother. In this archetype, the proper role of the mother is self-sacrifice for her children. Using language and concepts developed by Freud and Lacan, Sarah Arnold describes the contrast between the Good and Bad mother: 'Maternal power is figured as violent, destructive, and detrimental to the child. The Good Mother, on the other hand, recognizes the Law of the Father as legitimate' (Arnold, 2013: 11). Rather than asserting her own will, this Good Mother subordinates her sense of self to the father's vision of the family, giving up her own desires to support her husband and raise their children.

Increasingly, this idea has come under critique in contemporary horror films. Elsewhere, I have written about the use of these images of the Good and Bad mother in the French film *Inside* (2008), in which the woman coded as the Bad mother is the film's protagonist, and the Good mother is depicted as monstrous (Grafius, 2015). Sarah Arnold has also offered a provocative re-reading of David Cronenberg's *The Brood* (1979), focusing on the emotional pathos the film feels for the mother instead of her monstrous characteristics (Arnold, 2013: 79-90[4]). Similarly, *The Witch* presents Katherine as a sympathetic character, but reveals that her efforts to be the Good Mother are fruitless. Through the film, we see Katherine gradually become consumed by her anger over the insufficiency of her efforts as Mother, and the mistakes of her husband and oldest daughter. The film reveals that the expectations of the Good Mother are not attainable for anyone, even a maternal figure who tries as hard as Katherine.

An interesting insight into Katherine's character outside of her role as mother comes in the form of her missing silver cup. The viewer learns of it before Katherine mentions it; while William and Caleb are checking their traps in the forest, William mentions that he traded Katherine's silver cup for the traps. Katherine first asks Thomasin what she's done with it – assuming Thomasin is the guilty one within the family, even at this early stage of the film. When Thomasin replies that she thought it was on the shelf, Katherine says, 'It's been disappeared for some while.' In this small sentence, easily missed in the conversation, Katherine reveals herself to be someone who tries as hard as she can to ignore her own needs. It's only after the cup's disappearance has eaten away at her 'for some while' that Katherine is able to voice this loss. This exchange between Katherine and Thomasin also reveals the depth of the tension between these two characters. Katherine wonders how Thomasin could have lost it in such a small house, then sarcastically asks, 'Did a wolf vanish it too?', a vindictive reference to Thomasin having lost Samuel at the river's edge. For Katherine, Samuel's disappearance is not an unfortunate result of the family's precarious situation in the wilderness: it is Thomasin's fault. In this scene, Katherine's silver cup serves as a stand-in for her lost baby.

The silver cup is also tied to another longing on Katherine's part. At the dinner table, she mentions that it was her father's cup. In bed with William, shortly thereafter, he mentions the cup to her, as an example of luxuries they can do without. Katherine responds with frustration. 'It is not for vanity that I grieve of it,' she scolds William. But she catches herself before revealing why she does grieve for the cup; instead, she pauses, and shifts her line of conversation to lament that they were not able to sell the cup. The viewer must wait for later in the film to piece together what the silver cup does, in fact, mean to Katherine. As Caleb is lying on his death bed, Katherine laments the family's dire situation. William asks her what she wants. Katherine responds, half sobbing, 'I want to be home…in England.' Throughout the course of the film, her anger grows towards Thomasin for having lost Samuel, and towards William for taking them away from England. She tries to keep this anger inside, as part of her duty as the Good Mother, but eventually it explodes in rage at her husband and daughter.

Although it is not spoken of again, Katherine's silver cup returns once more in the film. Late at night, with William out chopping wood and the surviving children locked in the barn, Katherine slips out of bed and has her own encounter with the Devil. As she walks to the fireplace to light her candle, her eyes land on the silver cup, resting on a shelf. She quickly looks away from it, as her two dead children, Caleb and Samuel, call out to her. The Devil has tempted her with the two things she most desires: her children returned to her, and the silver cup as a symbol of home. These represent her dearest desires, and also the ruptures in her family that she cannot forgive.

After Black Phillip's murder of William, Katherine and Thomasin are the only two surviving members of the family. Katherine flies into a rage, believing Thomasin responsible for their deaths. In one of the film's most intensely emotional scenes, Katherine topples Thomasin to the ground, attempting to choke her to death. A crying Thomasin reaches for William's axe and strikes several blows to her mother, Katherine's blood falling on her. As Katherine dies on top of Thomasin, the camera pulls back, holding for several seconds on a still shot of the two women. While Katherine is lying dead on top of her daughter, the two women still seem as if they are locked in an embrace. Family bonds are hard to break; even in the midst of so much violence, tenderness isn't too far away.

JONAS AND MERCY

Jonas and Mercy are almost always shown together, and are seldom differentiated as characters. Even in the opening courtroom scene, when each of the family members is introduced with their own close-up, Jonas and Mercy are framed together. There are several exceptions to their pairing, one highly important one and two smaller ones which will be discussed below. But overall, these are the only characters in the family (with the exception of baby Samuel) whose function is primarily to advance the plot, rather than having a character arc of their own.

Mostly, Jonas and Mercy are seen in relation to Black Phillip. For most of the film, Phillip is viewed by the family as just one of their livestock. But Jonas and Mercy know better. We are first introduced to Phillip after he has escaped his pen, and Jonas and Mercy are following him around the yard. They sing an eerie song about Black Phillip, which includes the line: 'We are his servants, we are ye men, Black Phillip eats the lions from the lions' den.' While we are never led to understand how they came about this knowledge, they understand Phillip's true nature much earlier than the rest of the family.

Jonas and Mercy with their special friend (© A24)

The relationship between Jonas, Mercy, and Black Phillip becomes more chilling after Caleb's return, as he lies sick and dying in the family's cottage. A jump cut to an extreme close-up of Phillip's face moves the action into the barn, accompanied by the off-screen sounds of Mercy 'baa-ing' into Phillip's ear. She asks, 'What ails Caleb, Black Phillip? Did Thomasin make him sick in the woods?' Thomasin overhears this as she is milking another goat. 'Black Phillip says you are wicked,' Caleb asserts. Mercy continues, 'He says you put the devil in Caleb. That's why he's sick.' It is difficult to imagine these two young children making up these details out of whole cloth. Thomasin seems to know this; after her father accuses her of witchcraft, she immediately tries to turn the tables on Jonas and Mercy, pleading with William to pay attention to the unnatural relationship they have developed with the beast. Thomasin's argument is convincing enough that William locks all of the children in the barn, though Jonas and Mercy will not survive the night.

As stated above, Jonas and Mercy are usually paired together. One of the few exceptions is early in the film, in the scene by the riverbank. Mercy interrupts a tender moment between Thomasin and Caleb by pretending to be the witch. When Thomasin scolds her for being away from the farm on her own, Mercy responds, 'Black Phillip says I can do what I like,' again demonstrating a deeper understanding of Phillip than the other family members. In this scene, Mercy also claims to have seen the witch riding around the woods. While this scene has been discussed above from the perspective of Thomasin, it is also important to note Mercy's reaction. Mercy is in control of the situation as long as she asserts that the power of Black Phillip is on her side. She is also confident during her tale of having seen the witch; it is only when Thomasin claims that she herself is the witch that Mercy breaks into tears. Mercy's response remains ambiguous during this scene, which leads to two plausible readings. In the first, Mercy has been telling stories about Black Phillip and the witch, and believes none of what she says; she has been playing a children's game with her brother, but is terrified at the possibility that Thomasin speaks truth about being a witch. But in the second possible reading, Mercy speaks truly about her experience with Black Phillip, and possibly having seen the witch as well. As she has experienced the truth of these supernatural realities, her real terror lies in the possibility that Thomasin, as a powerful witch, would be hostile to her – not a friend like Black Phillip. Given that Mercy's understanding of Black Phillip proves prescient, this second reading seems to have more evidence to support it.

There are two other brief scenes that depict these characters apart from each other, both while Caleb is asleep after returning home from his encounter with the witch. First, we see William harvesting corn (in what seems to be labor almost as useless as his wood chopping), with Jonas silently looking on in the background. Immediately afterwards, the film cuts to Katherine, Thomasin, and Mercy shucking corn together. As they work, Mercy idly sings another creepy Black Phillip song. It begins, 'Black Phillip is a merry, merry king, he rules the land with mirth.' Again, Mercy's relationship with Black Phillip is emphasized, and she is proven to understand the animal's true nature, even as the rest of the family remains ignorant.

After Caleb vomits the apple while on his deathbed, the family is of one accord in viewing this as a sign of witchcraft. But Jonas and Mercy are the two who immediately blame Thomasin, telling their parents of all the oddities they have witnessed in her presence. In particular, they mention Samuel's disappearance while under her care and the goat whose milk turned to blood. But most damningly, Mercy tells the story of her encounter with Thomasin at the riverside, when Thomasin frightened Mercy into thinking that Thomasin herself was the witch of the woods. This is the accusation that sets the film's final, terrible events in motion.

As the film progresses, it seems more and more likely that Jonas and Mercy are, in fact, under the sway of Black Phillip. Part of their behavior might be a childish form of acting out, either with the intention of getting Thomasin in trouble or just because they're enjoying the attention. After they have accused Thomasin of witchcraft, William commands her to get on her knees. 'Love ye God?' he asks her. 'Love ye the Bible? Love ye prayer?' She is able, unhesitatingly, to answer 'yes' to each of these questions, a response which the annals of witch trials indicate an actual witch would not have been able to do. In contrast, when William attempts to lead the family in the Lord's Prayer, Jonas and Mercy 'cannot remember' the words, and are wracked with stomach pains. This is reminiscent of one of the 'tests' that New England courts would frequently use on the accused during witch trials. In a 1602 case of suspected witchcraft in London, an accused witch, Elizabeth Jackson, was forced to recite the Lord's Prayer as proof of her innocence. She omitted the words 'deliver us from evil', which was enough to convict her of witchcraft (Darr 2014: 156). Jonas and Mercy demonstrate this same inability to speak the Lord's Prayer. While in Jackson's case, the charge was clearly fabricated, in the

world of *The Witch* it provides solid evidence that Thomasin is right: Jonas and Mercy
have, indeed, been bewitched by Black Phillip. William recognizes the sign as important,
but reads it incorrectly. Instead of understanding it as indicating Jonas and Mercy's state
of bewitchment, he takes it to mean that Thomasin has bewitched the two of them.

Particularly when they are at Caleb's deathbed, Jonas and Mercy's actions seem similar
to the girls in the Salem courthouse, rolling on the floor and claiming they are actively
being bewitched by Thomasin. Furthermore, after Caleb cries out, 'She desires of my
blood!' the twins repeat this phrase, clearly marking their writhing as a performance.
Thomasin's response is clear: they are bewitched by Black Phillip, a view which Thomasin
will hold to the very end. When she summons Black Phillip after she has become the
only surviving family member, she asks him to speak to her as he does to Jonas and
Mercy. The Devil answers this request, seeming to confirm that Jonas and Mercy have
been speaking to him all along.

BLACK PHILLIP

While the previous section on the film's folkloric background has discussed the animal
imagery of *The Witch* more generally, Black Phillip is significant enough in the film that
he deserves to be treated along with the other characters. His presence looms large
enough over the film that he's taken on a cultural life of his own. New York rapper
Homeboy Sandman brags 'I'm like Black Phillip in a petting zoo' in his song 'Couple
Things', and for a while the goat had a fan-created Twitter handle. ('Living the delicious
life' was the account's tag line.) Several decades ago, Jeffrey Jerome Cohen noted in
regards to the monster that 'we envy it for its freedom' (1996: 17), and the cultural
response to Black Phillip bears this out.

Black Phillip is first seen running amok at the family's homestead, having escaped from
his pen while William and Caleb were off in the woods. At first, he is running ahead of
Jonas and Mercy, who chase him while singing their Black Phillip song, but as soon as
William returns Phillip challenges the patriarch's authority. He rears up on his hind legs,
menacing Jonas and Mercy, and William has to grab him by the horns to wrestle him
into his pen. William is successful in returning Phillip to his pen, but the struggle also

results in William being thrown to the ground, landing in a mud puddle. While the family will not recognize it until it is too late, this is the first indication that Black Phillip serves to disrupt the harmony that the family tries to achieve. Before his murder of William and climactic appearance as the devil, Black Phillip continually serves as a chaotic force within the family, exacerbating the fault lines that are already starting to spread.

Living deliciously (© A24)

The specific manner in which Black Phillip tries to pry the family apart is in the way he undermines both William and Kate in their role as parents. This is already present in the scene above, as Black Phillip manages to toss William in the mud before returning to his pen. It's also seen in how Black Phillip becomes an authority for Jonas and Mercy, replacing William and Kate as their moral guide. As Thomasin is washing her father's muddy clothes at the river, Mercy follows, pretending to be the witch. 'I'll tell mother you've left the farm alone.' Mercy responds indolently, 'Black Phillip says I can do what I like.' Mercy's parents are no longer her guardian; she takes orders from Black Phillip.

Much of the film is composed of medium-close shots of the characters, interspersed with longer medium shots in which two or more of the characters are present. The film's most extreme close-up involves a scene mid-way through the film, as Caleb lies on his deathbed. After William has gone outside to chop wood, a new scene starts with a jarring close-up of Black Phillip's face. The sound of 'baa-ing' is heard off-screen, and it is only after a couple of seconds that Mercy's face appears and we are able to identify her as the source of the sound. She bleats into Black Phillip's ear, while the goat stares on at the camera, eerily unmoved. Mercy asks why Caleb is ill. 'Did Thomasin make him sick in the woods?' she inquires of the goat. In this scene, it is clear that both Jonas and Mercy view Black Phillip as the source of knowledge, an authority they trust more than they trust anyone else in their family.

At the film's conclusion, Black Phillip follows Thomasin into the woods; after Thomasin has entered, he runs ahead of her, exiting the frame as Thomasin approaches the witches' Sabbath. As is the case in *The Witch*, black billy goats are frequently associated with the Devil in continental witchcraft lore. And in a similar vein to this final segment of *The Witch*, billy goats are often associated with bringing witches to their Sabbaths.

The records preserve an interrogation of a suspected witch from the German town of Blankenheim in 1627. The suspect was asked how she arrived at the witch's Sabbath; she responded that the 'evil one' had carried her on a 'white goat'. After taking a break to make sure her story conformed to the correct theological notions, she corrected her account to state that the Evil One carried her 'on a black billy goat' (de Blécourt: 2013, 94). So the idea of a goat as the Devil's familiar is one with a background in folk traditions; similarly, there are traditions of the demonic powers taking the form of a goat. Johannes Junius was executed for witchcraft in 1628. His primary crime was having sexual relations with a demon. According to Junius's confession, this demon appeared to him as a beautiful woman. After they had intercourse, his partner 'was transformed into a goat, which 'bleated' that it would break Johannes's neck unless he renounced God' (Stephens 2003: 5). From this perspective, Black Phillip is the latest in a long line of demonic, devil-associated goats.

FAMILY TROUBLES

In Robin Wood's article, 'The American Nightmare: Horror in the 70s' (Wood: 2003, 63-84), the critic famously argues that one of the major fault lines dividing earlier horror cinema with more modern iterations is the understanding of the family. In earlier horror films, such as the Universal classics of the '30s and '40s, the family was under attack from without, fighting for their survival against monsters who are usually coded as Other in some way or another (racial, religious, etc.). The family is the ideal state of the world, and one which must be protected at all costs. However, in the modern period (beginning with 1960's *Psycho*, and coming into full bloom with the 1968 double-header of *Rosemary's Baby* and *Night of the Living Dead*), horror films began to think of the family not as the ideal to be preserved, but as itself the source of evil. Rather than attacking the family from without, the monster comes from within.

The family of *The Witch* first thinks they are under this kind of assault from without, but belatedly realizes that the threat is actually of their own making. In essence, William misunderstands what kind of a horror movie he is in. While he thinks he's in Universal's 1931 version of *Dracula*, protecting his family from the scourge of the evil witch from the woods, he's actually in something akin to *Psycho*, in which it is the family itself who creates monsters.

Part of the success of *The Witch* is in the way it lays out the motivations, dreams, and desires of each of the family members so clearly. However, the structure of the family does not allow for the pursuit of these desires; instead, they must be suppressed for the good of the family. This fits particularly well with Eggers' Puritan context, but it is not unique to the 17th century – families today still function (to the extent that they do) through a process of each individual member repressing their own desires. The family as a whole is all that matters. The individual members are simply a cog in the family machine.

William has bought into this ideal so thoroughly that his individual desires are seldom articulated in the film, if at all. The only exception is his obstinance at the film's opening, when he refuses to recant in front of the Puritan tribunal. But from the context of the Puritan family, even this can be seen as a sacrifice – as head of the household, William is responsible for the spiritual life of his family members, including the state of their souls. Since William has repressed his own desires so thoroughly, we only see his frustrations as he is unable to protect and care for his family in the way he feels he is obligated to. With each of the family members, Thomasin and Katherine in particular, we see their frustrations boil over as their repression is unsuccessful. More than that, they gradually realize that their ideal of a family is unattainable, leading them to collapse rather than security and protection.

Through this examination of each family member's character development and arc, we have seen how each of them has their own individual desires, which they try to sublimate in service of the family. Thomasin expresses in prayer the desire to be an obedient daughter and faithful Christian, but her interaction with Black Phillip reveals the drive towards material goods and a more comfortable life. Caleb wants to grow into the family patriarch, but also harbors sexual desires which cannot be fulfilled within the confines of the family. Katherine believes that by committing herself completely to William's vision of a perfect family, she will be taken care of and her children will be kept safe. And William has bought into the familial ideology of his Puritan context so thoroughly that his only desire seems to be within his role of patriarch of the family, but as a patriarch who is successful in maintaining and leading a godly family who is kept safe from external threats and has their basic needs met. Throughout the film, these promises made by the ideology of the family unit are exposed as an impossible lie, one which instead leads the family to ruin. The external forces they fear are real, but these malevolent forces are only able to enter into the closed unit of the family once the individual members have fallen apart, victims of their impossible vision of perfection.

FOOTNOTES

1. Creed 1993: 73-83; Clover 1992: 21-65, discusses the frequent trope, found in films such as *The Exorcist* (1973), of the young woman whose body is a perfect vessel for evil forces.

2. Of course, the type of fruit in the Garden of Eden is never specified in the story of Genesis, but is only described generically as 'fruit.' Apples were not known in the Middle East at the time of Genesis's composition, so the fruit the author had in mind is much more likely to have been a pomegranate. The association with apples didn't become common until the early 16th century. A brief history is provided in Martyris 2017.

3. Mather 2000: 298. This excerpt is taken from Mather's *Ornaments for the Daughters of Zion*, originally published in 1692.

4. This reading contrasts the influential reading of Creed 1993: 43-58, who focuses primarily on the abjection of the woman's body.

READINGS

THE TITLE

The film's first sleight-of-hand is with its title. The history of horror films is rife with movies named after their monstrous antagonist, going at least as far back as *Nosferatu*. The Universal cycle of horror films that began in the 1930s solidified this trend, with franchises in short succession being named after the villain: *Dracula* (1931), *The Mummy* (1932), *The Wolf-Man* (1941), *The Creature from the Black Lagoon* (1954). *Frankenstein* (1931) is a notable exception, especially to the extent one considers Victor Frankenstein to be the 'hero' of the film, but even this exception might explain the frequency with which Frankenstein's monster is referred to as simply 'Frankenstein' in the popular lexicon. This practice continues through the 40's and into the science-fiction/horror films of the 50's, with titles such as *Them!* (1954) and *The Thing from Another World* (1951). John Carpenter's re-make shortens this title to simply *The Thing* (1982), and the *Alien* (1979-) series continues in the same vein. Closer to contemporary times, we find titles such as *The Woman in Black* (2012), *The Babadook* (2014), *Annabelle* (2014), and *It* (Part 1: 2017; Part 2: 2019), all of them hinting at the monstrous presence which will haunt the film.

Two other formulations dominate horror titles: those centered on the film's location, and those centered on an event or action. Location titles include such well-known films as *The Last House on the Left*, *Crimson Peak*, and *The Cabin in the Woods*. In these films, the title draws attention to the centrality of the location in the film's narrative; frequently, this location and its history will be more important than the entities that haunt it. (For an excellent overview of location in the gothic tradition and the horror film, see Curtis 2008.) Event-based titles, while less common, emphasize the action inherent in the film, often with a direct or implied warning. These would include *Don't Look Now* (1973), and *Get Out!* (2017). There's also a strain of titles which attempt to invoke a mood, but are often so generic as to be interchangeable, with recent entries including *Insidious* (2010), *Sinister* (2012), and *The Conjuring* (2013).

Very few horror movies are named for the film's protagonist. One more recent exception appears to be Ti West's slow-burn ghost story *The Innkeepers* (2011). This creaky house narrative is set in a historical downtown hotel, which has rumored to have been haunted for generations. With fewer and fewer guests to keep them occupied, the hotel's owner has decided to close down; the desk clerks decide to occupy themselves during their last few days of employment by documenting the presence of ghosts. Since these two hotel clerks are the focus, it seems as if the title refers to them. But they are hourly workers, not the owners of the hotel; the actual owner never appears on screen. However, by the end of the film it becomes clear that the true innkeepers are not the human protagonists, but the ghosts who haunt the inn. While the film initially appears to be named for its protagonists, by the end it has become clear that it is, in fact, named for the malevolent ghosts.

Sarah Stephens as a young incarnation of the witch of the woods (© A24)

A more well-known exception is *The Exorcist* (1973). While clearly named after the film's protagonist, the title also intends to invoke a sense of menace and danger, as the protagonist's role in this frightening and arcane ritual is being highlighted. Another contemporary example is *Abraham Lincoln: Vampire-Hunter* (2012), which clearly intends to provoke shock by juxtaposing a well-known historical figure with a fictional role as slaughterer of the undead. In both cases, the role of the protagonist is highlighted, including this role's relation to the horror and danger of the film's plot. (Other exceptions tend to fall within the realm of action-horror hybrids, such as *Constantine* [2005]; action films are much more frequently named for their protagonists.)

More unusual is the tact taken by *The Witch*. On a first viewing, the title seems to clearly refer to the malevolent entity that haunts the woods and threatens the family. We see the witch in several guises throughout the film, including the aged crone who ritually slaughters the family's baby, and the enticing young woman who seduces Caleb. But by the film's conclusion, we realize that Thomasin has become the witch, and claimed the mantle of the film's title.

This echoes with another sleight-of-hand the film plays with its audience. As has been discussed above, the film begins with the family's patriarch, William, being interrogated for his religious beliefs. His refusal to recant is what gets his family banished from the colony, and sets the events of the story in motion. In this initial scene, William is established as the centerpiece of the narrative, and the audience readily identifies with him as the protagonist. But slowly throughout the film, Thomasin assumes centerstage, until she has stolen the role of protagonist from her father. By the end of the film, it has clearly become her story. The film tells us this from the beginning, by giving Anya Taylor-Joy first billing for her role as Thomasin. In this sense, the film is indeed named for the menacing monster in the woods (the witch), but also for the film's protagonist, Thomasin.

A subtitle, *A New England Folk Tale*, appears on the film's title screen. This subtitle will also prove to be of great significance, as it serves to tie *The Witch* to the tradition of New England folk horror. As has been touched on earlier, this lineage is an important part of *The Witch*.

THEMES OF FOLK HORROR

If *The Witch* had been written with Scovell's template of the folk horror genre in mind, it could hardly have hewed more closely to the genre's markers. The rural setting in the distant past emphasizes the contrast in moral values; in *The Witch*, this system of religious and familial control will be explored through the storylines of each individual character, then revealed to be an impossible situation for them to thrive within. These moral values are laid out clearly in the character of William, then reflected in Caleb's imitation – Katherine and Thomasin suffer the brunt of the consequences. William's religious convictions first lead the family to be excommunicated and driven into the wilderness; through the course of the film, this sincere conviction will be critiqued and unmasked as a manifestation of stubborn pride. As William reveals in his prayers, his religious beliefs are inextricable from his pride. This initial decision reverberates throughout the film. Due to William's role as patriarch, the rest of his family is held hostage to his refusal to yield to the Colony's authorities. This cycle continues with Caleb, who learns from his father the art of repression, and the art of lying. It's a cycle which all of the family are trapped within, unable to resist the authority which Puritan society has granted William as the head of the household.

Isolation is also front and center in *The Witch*, with the family's mistrust of each other only growing because William is unwilling to go into town for help. On a deeper level, their isolation causes them to point the finger at each other when things start to go horribly wrong, another cycle which will only make their problems worse. Like horror classics of isolation such as *The Thing* and *The Shining*, the family is left with no one to rely upon but themselves. In the end, their isolation feeds into their desperation, serving as one of the elements that makes them a perfect target for the evil that lurks in the woods.

Of course, the landscape plays as large a part in *The Witch* as it does in *The Wicker Man*, or *Witchfinder General*, or any other entry into the folk horror genre. The woods are an ever-present danger, a constant reminder that the family is alone and unsafe. While William may boast that they will beat the woods, there's little conviction behind this sentiment – none of the family members believes it. Eggers emphasizes this menace through the association of the woods with unsettling choral music, through the moving camera that seems to watch the family from within the woods, and through the family's sense of ever-present danger that emanates from the forest. This danger only increases when the witch comes out of the woods to steal Samuel away, and we know that the family's fear of their surroundings is not an exaggeration. The woods are full of evil.

And finally, the film leads inevitably to Thomasin's pact with the Devil, a summoning which has been hinted at throughout the film. After Black Phillip has killed William, and Katherine lies dead by Thomasin's hand, there is little else for the film's protagonist to do than to sign the book that has been waiting for her from the beginning. As Scovell discusses in his analysis of folk horror, this meeting was inevitable. The film has been leading us towards this all along.

RE-THINKING WITCHES

The film's ending forces a re-evaluation of many of the concepts the film has been employing throughout. First among these is the very idea of witches.

As has been explored earlier, the history of 'witchcraft', until very recently when the term has been at least partially reclaimed, is a history of women's oppression, religious anxiety, and finding scapegoats to blame for everyday calamities. Patriarchal authorities have used the concept of 'witchcraft' as a means of controlling and punishing women who do not adhere to the community's rules in the proper manner, particularly when the transgressions are nebulously defined. The community might not be quite sure what she's done (other than make them uncomfortable), but if they call her a witch, the whole community will rally against her. It's an efficient way to maintain control over women who might be too free-spirited or otherwise troublesome.

From this perspective, there were no witches in Salem, or in Europe previously. There were only ordinary women whom the community's authorities wanted to keep in line, or use as an example for other women. (Don't cause trouble, or this might happen to you, too!) Midnight sabbaths were a fiction of the male imagination, and there was no devil looking for consorts, only the patriarchal authorities. Rather than emerging from the world of the supernatural, witches emerged as an answer to the question of 'How can we best exert control over women, and make ourselves feel better about the problems in our lives?'

The Witch complicates this picture; while Thomasin is clearly the film's protagonist, and the patriarchal worldview of William has ruptured, the film's conclusion pulls another surprise by revealing that there really is a devil behind these events, there really was a witch in the woods, and Thomasin really does join a coven of witches. What started out as William's paranoid fantasy about his daughter becomes a reality. But the film is able to use this foray into the supernatural as yet another means of critiquing patriarchal worldviews and family structures.

Another recent film dealing with witchcraft, though more obliquely, provides an interesting point of comparison. In *The Conjuring*, a 'typical' American family is haunted by the spirits dwelling in their old farmhouse. They gradually learn that the evil behind all of the hauntings is the ghost of Bathsheba, one of the farmhouse's original residents and a descendant of one of the witches burned at Salem. Bathsheba became possessed by the devil and murdered her child; she was hung by the townspeople outside of the house, but continues to haunt the property. While *The Conjuring* has much to commend it, this backstory is rather problematic.

Through Bathsheba's backstory, *The Conjuring* implies several things about witches. Most obviously, Bathsheba is associated with witchcraft and devil worship; these two categories seem to be blurred together. Bathsheba's identity as a witch is indistinguishable from her role as evil presence. Furthermore, by grounding Bathsheba's past in the Salem witches, the strong implication is that the Salem witches, too, were evil beings possessed by the Devil. In this worldview, Judge Hathorne and his fellow witch-hunters were not paranoid men wrapped up in their own power, but righteous crusaders who understood the true nature of evil. It's not a positive picture of witchcraft, or women in general.

The Witch is much more subtle in its treatment of witches. The witch in the woods is an evil presence, and the devil is behind all of the witchery we have witnessed on-screen. But the character of Thomasin provides a significant complication to the simple equation offered by *The Conjuring*. As we have explored earlier, while all of the family have an interior life of their own, Thomasin is the center of the film's sympathy. She remains a sympathetic character to the end, even as she signs her name in the devil's book and dances with the other witches in the woods. How is this possible? The answer lies in the film's final image, depicting Thomasin's overwhelming joy as she floats into the air.

THE FINAL SCENE: THOMASIN'S LAUGHTER

The final scene of *The Witch* has polarized viewers. For some, it reveals too much; more chilling would have been to leave Thomasin walking into the woods with Black Phillip, the actual presence of witches left to the viewer's imagination. But for others, it ties together the film's themes perfectly, and provides a necessary level of grounding for what has been, up until this point, a highly ambiguous film. In the reading I offer below, this ending is crucial to resolving the conflicts within the film.

After Thomasin signs her contract with Black Philip, now revealed as the Devil, she undresses, and slowly leaves the settlement to walk into the woods. The camera remains in a static longshot as Thomasin walks across the field and between the trees. I've spoken to more than one viewer who wished the film had ended there; instead, we follow Thomasin into the woods, where she is drawn to a roaring fire, surrounded by naked witches. As they dance around the fire, they begin to levitate, and Thomasin laughs gleefully. The film ends on a close-up of her laughing face.

Thomasin gets the last laugh (© A24)

While the desire for the film to end with Thomasin walking into the woods is understandable from a dramatic standpoint (the image of her slowly walking into the previously forbidden forest is extremely chilling), the image of Thomasin's laughter provides the film with a thematic closure that would have been missing otherwise. There is so little joy in this film; to end on a close-up of a laughing face is striking.

French theorist Hélène Cixous, in her oft-cited article 'The Laugh of the Medusa', explores the idea of women's writing as a way to reclaim a sense of self and redefine the individual as subject against the constrictions of patriarchal culture. In this 'feminine writing', Cixous identifies woman's laughter as an expression of self that cannot be controlled. As a result, laughter is a challenge to patriarchal control, and an expression of woman's individuality. Cixous writes, 'You only have to look at the Medusa straight on to see her. And she's not deadly. She's beautiful, and she's laughing' (Cixous 1976, 885).

In the final scene of *The Witch*, Thomasin embodies Cixous's laughing Medusa. There has been nothing but dour events throughout the film, and Thomasin has had few opportunities to laugh. Perhaps the only other instance of Thomasin's laughter in the film is in the much earlier scene when she torments her little sister by pretending to be a witch herself; in this early scene, Thomasin has claimed this mantle of the witch for her own, and her laughter is a laughter of freedom and power. But through the rest of the film, denied access to agency or power, the option of laughter is denied to her. It is only when she has rejected the religious restrictions of her family and left the homestead that she is able to re-connect with this laughter.

The concluding close-up of Thomasin's laughing face also brings to mind another film, also about witchcraft (and also a major milestone in the folk horror genre): Michael Reeves's notoriously nasty 1968 film *Witchfinder General*. Vincent Price plays the titular Witchfinder, based on the historical figure Matthew Hopkins. In Reeves's film, Hopkins is less concerned with actually finding witches than he is with enacting his sadistic fantasies, and using his power as witchfinder to extract sexual favors from young women. One of the women abused by Hopkins is Sara, whose fiancé Marshall has tracked the witchfinder across the English countryside on a single-minded quest for revenge. In the climactic scene, Sara has been bound up for torture by Hopkins, when Marshall bursts in to save her by levelling her tormentor with an axe. (It's difficult to tell whether this axe should be classified as broad or narrow.) As the young man reigns blow after blow upon the malevolent witchfinder, Sara is not relieved to be rescued, but horrified at the cycle of violence she has been caught in. The film ends with a close-up of her scream (Cooper 2011: 70-73).

When juxtaposed with one another, Thomasin's laughter and Sara's scream tell two sides of the same story. Sara screams because she is caught within the repetition of patriarchal violence, a helpless pawn in a game played between two brutal men. Thomasin, in contrast, laughs out of the sheer exuberance she feels at being freed from the patriarchal restrictions of her family. Screaming is Sara's response to her realization that she is stuck as a victim – whether she is saved by her fiancé or not, she is still unable to escape from this economy of violence. But Thomasin laughs, knowing that she has freed herself from the stifling, overbearing structure of her family and their religious tradition.

Patriarchal violence and the scream in Witchfinder General *(© Tigon)*

Uncomfortably, the film leaves us with the image of female freedom as being linked to Thomasin's witch's pact with the devil. Following the logic of the film to its conclusion, we are left with the realization that Thomasin's only hope for escape was in rejecting her own family and tradition, and throwing her lot in with the devil. Remind me – where do we find evil?

So witches are real, the devil is real, and Thomasin is a witch who has given herself to the devil. But her father has charged her with witchcraft throughout the film, long before she signed the Black Book. While Thomasin becomes a witch in the end, this is a result of the charges of witchcraft and the crumbling patriarchal structure of her family. Thomasin would have preferred to find a family structure in which to live with her family members in peace; throughout the film, we have seen this denied to her. In the end, the witch's pact was the only choice left to Thomasin.

CONCLUSION

THE WITCH'S INFLUENCE

Four years after the release of *The Witch*, we're starting to see the influence it has had on the landscape of horror. In the discussion of genre, we have seen how *The Witch* was one of the first art-house horror films of the decade to be taken seriously by critics and scholars, while simultaneously succeeding at the box office. While teen horror is still an enormous money-maker for studios (Blumhouse seems to release a new film every other week, both in theaters and on streaming services), more and more horror films are being marketed towards adult audiences. *The Witch* is one of the main instigators of this trend.

But where we see *The Witch's* influence most directly is in the crop of folk horror and period horror films that began to emerge in 2018. Whether these films were directly inspired by *The Witch* or had been long-simmering projects that were finally able to find funding after the success of *The Witch* is difficult to say, but it doesn't seem accidental that these similarly themed films began to appear three years after *The Witch*.

The Golem (2018), based on Jewish folklore, features a 17th century setting that owes a good deal to *The Witch's* much-praised production design. While not featuring the isolation that drove the tension of *The Witch*, the film focuses on supernatural intrusions into family life, and how difficult belief systems can be to maintain in the midst of danger. It also centers on a young woman, though here a married mother rather than an adolescent, who finds herself stifled by her community and transgresses its boundaries.

The anthology film *The Field Guide to Evil* (2018) is an international production, featuring eight short films crafted by notable horror directors, each centered on folk tales from their native country. Several of the segments seem directly inspired by *The Witch*, particularly the opening short film from Austrian co-directors Veronika Franz and Severin Fiala (most well-known for the highly creepy 2015 film *Goodnight Mommy* and the 2019 film *The Lodge*). Entitled 'The Sinful Women of Höllfall', this tale is set in a rural village, in an unspecified timeframe that seems like the 17th century. Aside from the time period and rural setting, it shares with *The Witch* a young female protagonist, Valerie, who struggles with how to live out her desires within the confines of a repressive family environment. In this short film, the family is not in opposition to the supernatural force, but the demonic presence reinforces the conservative sexual values of the family by attacking young women who exhibit any unsanctioned sexual desires. Like Thomasin, Valerie takes matters into her own hands, defeating the demon so she can pursue carnal relations with the young woman next door.

Recent years have seen a resurgence in period-horror, which also seems due to the success of *The Witch*. Most notable are the folk-inspired *The Wind* (2018), set in the 19th century American frontier, and *The Isle* (2018), employing Scottish folklore to provide the scares for its Victorian-era setting. *The Wind*, in particular, seems to have been influenced by *The Witch*. It centers on frontier couple Lizzy and Isaac, living miles away from civilization or even other homesteads. Lizzy's isolation grows as Isaac heads to town for supplies, and she begins to suspect that there is something unnatural about the landscape, and, in particular, the wind. While the attention to period detail is several notches below that of *The Witch*, the similarities in plot structure, tone, and subtext are readily apparent. Also noteworthy is *The Nightingale* (2019), Jennifer Kent's follow-up to *The Babadook*. It's a revisionist mash-up of rape-revenge and Western tropes, stirred together to provide a critique of Australia's colonial past, also set in the 19th century. While it's lack of supernatural or folkloric elements cause it to be several steps removed from *The Witch*, the period setting and careful attention to set design makes it feel like the two films have some kinship. Eggers' film casts a shadow over all of these productions, and audiences and critics alike are liable to have *The Witch* in mind while watching them.

Robert Eggers' follow-up film *The Lighthouse* (2019) works with many of the same ideas as *The Witch*, even if audiences and critics didn't feel as if it quite captured the horrifying magic of its predecessor. This second feature-film concerns two men stationed at an isolated lighthouse, young and troubled Ephraim (Robert Pattinson) and grizzled veteran Thomas (Willem Dafoe). While it takes place several hundred years later than *The Witch*, *The Lighthouse* shares the New England setting and the sense of isolation with its predecessor. As the two men grow increasingly hostile and despairing, mythic elements such as libidinous mermaids and a sea monster appear with increasing intensity, and the situation spirals into the same kind of violence that marks the ending of *The Witch*. Unlike the clarity with which The Witch concludes, how much of *The Lighthouse*'s occurrences were the product of Ephraim's fever dream remains open to question. *The Lighthouse* shows evidence of a filmmaker still circling around a similar set of themes. It makes an excellent pairing with *The Witch*, with a large number of resonances and thematic connections, and also suggests a filmmaker whose oeuvre will continue to develop with multiple lines of interconnection between each individual movie.

PURITAN ANXIETIES, 20TH CENTURY FEARS

But what about *The Witch* has inspired these films? What in Eggers' film have filmmakers found worthy of trying to capture, and audiences wanting to seek more of?

Perhaps part of it is the way that Eggers' film feels both completely committed to its 17th century setting, yet also remarkably contemporary in the fears, anxieties, and hopes that its characters display. These characters are so distant from us, in their worldview, their manner of speech, the way they engage with their environment, and the role religion plays in their lives. But somehow, as an audience we're able to feel a connection with them. This speaks both to the skill with which Eggers has written these characters, giving each of them a complex series of motivations and flaws, as well as to the powerful performances given by the actors. Especially given the period dialect in which the actors were asked to speak, false notes would ring loudly. To my ears at least, as well as the ears of many others, the film doesn't strike any, but remains pitch perfect throughout in both writing and performance.

In *The Witch*, Eggers has found a way to burrow into the particular fears of these vivid, fully drawn Puritan characters, but in such a way that their terrors are still with us in the present day. We can't help but admire William for his unwavering faith and his refusal to compromise, even if his religious beliefs aren't ones that we hold. But we also know the fears of a family falling apart, and trying to hold everything together when it seems like there aren't any friends to be found. And we know the feelings of Katherine, trying to support her family but realizing that it may be beyond saving, and that her steadfastness has been for naught. And we understand Thomasin deeply, trying so hard to be the good daughter, the good person, that supports her family and puts their needs first, but worrying that she can only push her own desires down for so long. These characters are so easy for us to recognize in ourselves, even across the centuries.

Elsewhere, I've written about how this film (along with *It Comes at Night*, 2017) reveals contemporary anxieties about borders and security (Grafius, 2019b). In both films, the family feel threatened by a force from without. In each case, they respond by trying to circle the wagons, by relying on themselves and shutting out the rest of the world. And in both films, this attempt is ultimately fruitless, as the families fall apart from within. In times of heightened anxiety, groups often respond by looking for scapegoats and trying to tighten the boundaries around themselves – this is true whether the group in question is a family, a church, or a nation. Usually, when one group starts attacking another, you can bet that there's some underlying insecurity that's causing the attacks.

We see this dramatized in *The Witch*, and it's a dramatization that strikes a chord with many of us. Most of us can look back at times in our own lives when we've participated in that kind of scapegoating, even if on small levels. And it's easy to look around at Western culture's fear of immigrants and recognize the same dynamic at play. While 17th century New England is several centuries and a world away, it's a world that still speaks to us.

America, in particular, has always had a complex relationship with the Puritans. While the country traces much of its religious and cultural heritage back to this group, we're also appalled at their severe judgmental streak, and the way in which they seemed to turn life into nothing but dour, strict rule-following. However, America still prides itself on inheriting the work ethic of its colonial forebears, a work ethic which is often traced back to the Puritans in the cultural imagination. And the judgmental streak we decry in the Puritans is still a prominent feature of American culture. (Along with many others, of course.) Perhaps more than that, many of the questions which came to the forefront of Puritan faith, and which are depicted so clearly in *The Witch*, are questions that follow us through life, regardless of our own religious convictions or lack thereof. Just as William leads his family in worrying about whether their behaviors (and even thoughts) are good enough to be deemed acceptable, those of us in the 21st century also worry about whether we're good enough to succeed in the increasingly bleak landscape of late capitalism, a landscape in which the divide between the winners and losers is starker than ever. And we worry about the divide between the people we feel we're supposed to be, and the places that our wishes and desires might lead us to instead.

One of the questions the Puritans wrestled with was whether an individual could influence his or her salvation by his actions. They wanted to say no, salvation was entirely up to God. But they kept pushing back against this line, they kept trying to assert that there was some way in which their actions mattered. (As discussed earlier, this was the main complaint Anne Hutchinson had with the Puritan clergy – while trying to hold onto Calvin's doctrine that salvation was entirely up to God, they continued to find ways to insert human action into the equation.) Capitalism offers a similar dynamic to many of us today: we want to pretend that we live in a meritocracy, where those who are hard-working, skilled, and make good choices are rewarded. The fear is that this is untrue, that the economic system has been rigged in favor of those who already have, against those who don't. It's this creeping unease, this fundamental feeling that all is not right, that has led (or at least contributed) to the rise of reactionary populist movements across the West.

Thomasin triumphant (© A24)

The Puritans in general, and the family in *The Witch* in particular, approach this problem from different perspectives than most of us do in the 21st century. For them, the question was how their actions could matter in the face of God's inscrutable will and complete control over the fate of the individual. They tried all sorts of ways to convince themselves that their choices still had meaning, which we see reflected in the theological pretzels of many of the sermons of the time. And we see it in William's assertion that Caleb was not damned because of his yielding to temptation, but that he was instead saved by his calling for Christ on his deathbed. While earlier, William's theology had told him that he could have no knowledge of Samuel's ultimate fate, this was not sufficient when faced with the death of his eldest son. In the case of William, his compassion and emotional connection for his son overrode his cold theological convictions. He had to convince himself that Caleb's deathbed repentance was meaningful. In a similar way, we weave myths about the opportunities in our society, and the possibility of creating a comfortable, happy life for ourselves and our families through the (Puritan-inspired) virtues of hard work and loyalty to our company. While we know how impossible it really is to pull ourselves up by our boot straps or make meaningful changes to our situation in life, we hold onto myths of success that tell us otherwise. But somewhere in the back of our minds, we worry that they're a lie.

We worry that, increasingly, we are asked to show loyalty to our employers, but receive none in return. We worry that the structures of taxation and finance are so skewed towards the already wealthy that we have no chance of improving our station in life more than the smallest amount. In effect, we worry that none of what we do matters. *The Witch* speaks directly to this anxiety, and works to build a bridge across the centuries through these shared fears over the potential meaninglessness of our lives. Whether we are consigned to our fate by a God whose motives we cannot understand, or by the caprices of an economic system that sometimes seems to only care for the well-off, it is terrifying to think that we might not be in control of our lives.

And this is why Thomasin's choice at the end is so powerful. It offers a conflicting set of emotions to the viewer, as horror often does. On the one hand, we sympathize with the box she has found herself in, a confined family structure that offers her no room to move, to grow, or to make her own decisions. We sympathize with her feelings of helplessness and frustration. We sympathize with her inability to make her own choices, to give her life the meaning she decides to give to it. But when she pushes outside of these structures, it is through a horrifying act of violence (even if in self-defense), and a pact with the very embodiment of evil. Is this the only choice we are offered? Either to suffer through an utter lack of control in our lives, or to throw our lot in with evil? *The Witch* doesn't offer easy answers. But it raises the questions in powerful ways, and reminds us of how high the stakes are. Whether it's a 17th century Puritan family or our own lives today, our fears and our dreams share much in common.

BIBLIOGRAPHY

Almond, P (2014) *The Devil: A New Biography.* Ithaca, NY: Cornell University Press.

Altman, R (1999) *Film/Genre.* London: BFI Publishing.

Arnold, S (2013) *Maternal Horror Film: Melodrama and Motherhood.* London: Palgrave MacMillan.

Bakhtin, M. (1981) *The Dialogic Imagination: Four Essays by M. M. Bakhtin.* Caryl Emerson and Michael Holquist, trans. Austin: University of Texas Press.

Barbera, J. (2019) 'The Id Follows: *It Follows* (2014) and the Existential Crisis of Adolescent Sexuality', *International Journal of Psychoanalysis* (100.2), pp. 393-404.

Bettenson, H. and C. Maunder, eds. (2011) *Documents of the Christian Church.* 4th edition. London: Oxford University Press.

Bever, E. (2013) 'Popular Witch Beliefs and Magical Practices'. In: Levack, B. P., ed, *The Oxford Handbook of Witchcraft in Early Modern Europe and Colonial America.* London: Oxford University Press, pp. 50-68.

Bigsby, C. (2003) 'Introduction'. In: Miller, Arthur, *The Crucible.* New YorkL Penguin Books, pp. vii-xxv.

Briefel, A. (2019) 'The Devil in the Details: The Uncanny History of *The Witch*'. *Film and History* (49.1), pp. 4-20.

Buscombe, E. (1995) 'The Idea of Genre in the American Cinema'. In: Grant, B. K. ed., *Film Genre Reader II.* Austin: University of Texas Press, pp. 11-25.

Carden, A. (1990) *Puritan Christianity in America: Religion and Life in Seventeenth-Century Massachusetts.* Grand Rapids, MI: Baker Book House.

Cixous, H. (1976) 'The Laugh of the Medusa'. *Signs* (1.4), pp. 875-893.

Cohen, J. J. 'Monster Culture (Seven Theses)'. In: Cohen, J. J., ed, *Monster Theory: Reading Culture.* Minneapolis: University of Minnesota Press, pp. 3-25.

Cohn, N. 'The Non-Existent Society of Witches'. In: Bradshaw, E. G., ed, *Witches of the Atlantic World: A Historical Reader and Primary Sourcebook*. New York: New York University Press, pp. 49-59.

Cooper, I. (2011) *Witchfinder General*. Devil's Advocates. Leighton Buzzard, UK: Auteur Publishing.

Cowan, D. E. (2018) *America's Dark Theologian: The Religious Imagination of Stephen King*. New York: New York University Press.

Creed, B. (1993) *The Monstrous-Feminine: Film, Feminism, Psychoanalysis*. London: Routledge.

Curtis, B. (2008) *Dark Places: The Haunted House in Film*. London: Reaktion Books.

Darr, O. A. (2014) 'Experiments in the Courtroom: Social Dynamics and Spectacles of Proof in Early Modern English Witch Trials'. *Law & Social Inquiry* (39.1), pp. 152-175.

de Blécourt, W. (2013) 'Sabbath Stories: Towards a New History of Witches' Assemblies'. In: Levack, B. P., ed, *The Oxford Handbook of Witchcraft in Early Modern Europe and Colonial America*. London: Oxford University Press, pp. 84-100.

Dowley, T. (2018) *Introduction to the History of Christianity*. Third Edition. Minneapolis: Fortress Press.

Duca, L. (2016) 'How Robert Eggers Wove the Nightmares of *The Witch* Out of Historical Documents'. [online] *Vulture*. Available at https://www.vulture.com/2016/02/how-robert-eggers-researched-the-witch.html [Accessed 8 January, 2020].

Ebiri, B. (2014) '*Under the Skin*, *The Only Lovers Left Alive*, and a Brief History of the Art-House Horror Film'. [online] https://www.vulture.com/2014/04/under-the-skin-and-a-history-of-art-horror-film.html [Accessed 13 April, 2020].

Francis, R. (2005) *Judge Sewall's Apology: The Salem Witch Trials and the Forming of a Conscience*. New York: Fourth Estate.

Frow, J. (2015) *Genre*, 2nd edition. London and New York: Routledge.

Galambush, J. (2018) *Reading Genesis: A Literary and Theological Commentary. Reading the Old Testament*. Macon: Smyth & Helwys.

Gaustad, E. and L. Schmidt (2002) *The Religious History of America: The Heart of the American Story from the Colonial Times to Today.* New York: HarperOne.

Godbeer, R. (1992) *The Devil's Dominion: Magic and Religion in Early New England.* New York: Cambridge University Press.

González, J. L. (2010) *The Story of Christianity, Volume 2: The Reformation to the Present Day.* Revised and Updated edition. New York: HarperOne.

Grafius, B. R. (2015) *Ideas of Motherhood* in Inside, *Horror Studies* (6.1), pp. 57-68.

Grafius, B. R. (2019a) *Reading the Bible with Horror*, Lanham, MD: Lexington Books/ Fortress Academic.

Grafius, B. R. (2019b) 'Securing the Borders: Isolation and Anxiety in *The Witch, It Comes at Night*, and Trump's America'. In: McCollum, V., ed, *Make America Hate Again: Trump-Era Horror and the Politics of Fear.* London: Routledge, pp. 119-128.

Hamori, E. J. (2013) 'The Prophet and the Necromancer: Women's Divination for Kings'. *Journal of Biblical Literature* (132.4), pp. 827-843

Hawthorne, N. (2011) *Hawthorne's Short Stories.* Edited and with an introduction by Newton Arvin. New York: Vintage.

Hawthorne, N. (2014) *The Scarlett Letter: A Romance.* Vintage Classics Edition. New York: Vintage.

Ifeanyi, K. C. (2016) 'Anatomy of a Scene: The Most Pivotal Moment in 'The Witch', Explained'. *Fast Company.* [online] Available at https://www.fastcompany.com/3056743/ anatomy-of-a-scene-the-most-pivotal-moment-in-the-witch-explained [Accessed 8 January, 2020].

Ingebretsen, E. (1996) *Maps of Heaven, Maps of Hell: Religious Terror as Memory from the Puritans to Stephen King.* London: M. E. Sharpe.

Jagendorf, M. (1948) *New England Bean-Pot: American Folk Stories to Read and to Tell.* New York: Vanguard Press.

Kieckhefer, R (2013) 'The First Wave of Trials for Diabolical Witchcraft'. In: Levack, B. P., ed, *The Oxford Handbook of Witchcraft in Early Modern Europe and Colonial America.*

London: Oxford University Press, pp. 159-178.

LaPlante, E. (2004) *American Jezebel: The Uncommon Life of Anne Hutchinson, the Woman Who Defied the Puritans*. San Francisco: HarperSanFrancisco.

Lloyd, C. (2019) "I Told You Not to Go into That House': *Get Out* and Horror's Racial Politics'. In: McCollum, V., ed, *Make America Hate Again: Trump-Era Horror and the Politics of Fear*. London: Routledge, pp. 109-118.

Matther, C. (2000) 'The Character of a Virtuous Woman'. In: Breslaw, E. G., ed., *Witches of the Atlantic World: A Historical Reader and Primary Sourcebook*. New York: New York University Press, pp. 296-299.

Miller, A. (2003) *The Crucible: A Play in Four Acts*. With an introduction by Christopher Bigsby. New York: Penguin, 2003.

Moore, J. P. jr. (2005) *Prayer in America: A Spiritual History of Our Nation*. New York: Doubleday.

Morgan, E. S. (1966) *The Puritan Family: Religion and Domestic Relations in Seventeenth-Century New England*. Revised and Enlarged Edition. Westport, CT: Greenwood Press.

Murphy, M. (2016) 'That (Very, Very) Old Black Magic in 'The Witch''. *New York Times*. [online] Available at https://www.nytimes.com/2016/02/21/movies/the-witch-movie-production-design.html [Accessed 19 January, 2020].

Pagnattaro, Marisa Anne (2001) *In Defiance of the Law: From Anne Hutchinson to Toni Morrison*, New York: Peter Lang.

Parish, H. (2019) "Paltrie Vermin, Cats, Mise, Toads, and Weasils': Witches, Familiars, and Human-Animal Interactions in the English Witch Trials'. *Religions* (10.2), pp. 1-14.

Phesant-Kellly, F. (2019) 'Trauma, Repression, and *The Babadook*: Sexual Identity in the Trump Era'. In: McCollum, V., ed, *Make America Hate Again: Trump-Era Horror and the Politics of Fear*. London: Routledge, pp. 81-94.

Poole, W. S. (2009) *Satan in America: The Devil We Know*. Lanham, MD: Rowman and Littlefield.

Proot, G. (2014) 'Miracles Lately Wrought: The Use of 'VV' for 'W' in 17th-century Titles'. *The Collation: Research and Exploration at the Folger*. [online] Available at: https://collation.folger.edu/2014/08/miracles-lately-vvrovght-the-use-of-vv-for-w-in-17th-century-titles/ [Accessed 30 April 2019].

Ray, B. C. (2010) "The Salem Witch Mania': Recent Scholarship and American History Textbooks'. *Journal of the American Academy of Religion* (78.1), pp. 40-64.

Ray, B. C. (2015) *Satan & Salem: The Witch-Hunt Crisis of 1692*. Charlottesville: University of Virginia Press.

Reynolds, L. J. (2008) *Devils & Rebels: The Making of Hawthorne's Damned Politics*. Ann Arbor, MI: The University of Michigan Press.

Richardson, J. (2003) *Possessions: The History and Uses of Haunting in the Hudson Valley*. Cambridge, MA: Harvard University Press.

Robischeaux, T (2013) 'The German Witch Trials'. In: Levack, B. P., ed, *The Oxford Handbook of Witchcraft in Early Modern Europe and Colonial America*. London: Oxford University Press, pp. 179-198.

Rosenthal, B., ed. (2009) *Records of the Salem Witch-Hunt*. New York: Cambridge University Press.

Rowlands, A (2013) 'Witchcraft and Gender in Early Modern Europe'. In: Levack, B. P., ed, *The Oxford Handbook of Witchcraft in Early Modern Europe and Colonial America*. London: Oxford University Press, pp. 449-467.

Rutkowski, P (2019) 'Animal Transformation in Early Modern English Witchcraft Pamphlets'. *Anglica* (28.1), pp. 21-34.

'Salem Witch Trials Documentary Archive'. [online] Available at: http://salem.lib.virginia.edu [Accessed 6 December 2019].

Schiff, S. (2015) *The Witches: Salem, 1692*. New York: Little, Brown and Company.

Scovell, A. (2017) *Folk Horror: Hours Dreadful and Things Strange*. Leighton Buzzard, UK: Auteur Publishing.

Shimabukuro, K. (2016) 'The Mystery of the Woods: *Twin Peaks* and the Folkloric Forest'. *Cinema Journal* 55.3: 121-125.

Silver, A. (1996) 'Introduction'. In: Silver, A., and Ursini, J., eds, *The Film Noir Reader*. New York: Limelight Editions, pp. 3-15.

Skal, D. J. (2001) *The Monster Show: A Cultural History of Horror*. Revised edition. New York: Faber & Faber.

Stephens, W. (2003) *Demon Lovers: Witchcraft, Sex, and the Crisis of Belief*. 2nd edition. Chicago: University of Chicago Press.

Stokes R. E. (2019) *The Satan: How God's Executioner Became the Enemy*, Grand Rapids, MI: Eerdmans.

Towlson, J. (2018) *Candyman*. Devil's Advocates. Leighton Buzzard, UK: Auteur Publishing.

Tudor, A. (1995) 'Genre'. In: Grant, B. K., ed., *Film Genre Reader II*. Austin: University of Texas Press, pp. 3-10.

Walsh, B. C. (2020) 'Colonising the Devil's Territories: The Historicity of Providential New England Folklore in *The Witch*'. *Revenant: Critical and Creative Studies of the Supernatural* 5.1, 144-166. [online] Available at: http://www.revenantjournal.com/wp-content/uploads/2020/03/8-Brendon-C-Walsh-1.pdf [Accessed 13 April, 2020].

Walton, S. (2018) 'Air, Atmosphere, Environment: Film Mood, Folk Horror, and *The Witch*'. *Screening the Past* 43. [online] Available at: http://www.screeningthepast.com/2018/02/air-atmosphere-environment-film-mood-folk-horror-and-the-witch/ [Accessed 15 December, 2019).

Wenzel, J. (2019) '*The Blair Witch Project* Was One of the Greatest Horror Hoaxes of the 20th Century'. [online] *Esquire*. Available at: https://www.esquire.com/entertainment/movies/a28381265/the-blair-witch-project-greatest-horror-real-hoax-20th-anniversary/ [Accessed 13 April, 2020].

Wiggins, S. A. (2018) *Holy Horror: The Bible and Fear in Movies*. Jefferson, NC: McFarland & Co.

Williams, T. (2014) *Hearths of Darkness: The Family in the American Horror Film*. Updated edition. Jackson, MS: University of Mississippi Press.

Winship, M. P. (2005) *The Times and Trials of Anne Hutchinson: Puritans Divided*. Lawrence: University Press of Kansas.

Winship, M. P. (2018) *Hot Protestants: A History of Puritanism in England and America*. New Haven: Yale University Press.

Wood, R. (2003) *Hollywood from Vietnam to Reagan…and Beyond*. New York: Columbia University Press.

Woodward, W. W. (2003) 'New England's Other Witch-Hunt: The Hartford Witch-Hunt of the 1660's and Changing Patterns in Witchcraft Prosecution'. *OAH Magazine of History* (17. 4), pp. 16-20.

Zlnoman, J. (2018) 'Home Is Where the Horror Is'. [online] *New York Times*. Available at https://www.nytimes.com/2018/06/07/movies/hereditary-horror-movies.html [Accessed 13 April 2020]

Printed and bound by CPI Group (UK) Ltd, Croydon, CR0 4YY

25/03/2025

14647350-0001